Three Perspectives on Customer Service

All You Have to Know

By

David Peters

Disclaimer

Every customer and situation is different so therefore it is impossible to create one universal approach that will work in any situation. Therefore it is the responsibility of the reader to determine which parts of this book, if any, are appropriate for use in any given situation and with any given individual. The writers, publishers and resellers of this book assume no responsibility for the use or application of any or all parts of this book.

Contents

A Note About this Book

This book is a collection of three other books each dealing with customer Service from each of three different viewpoints. There will be some duplication of content and similar topics of discussion throughout each volume.

While this might appear to be duplicate content it is actually the same content or aspect of customer service as seen by three different people.

Therefore the same topic will be presented in three different ways. This might help certain people understand things better or more in-depth.

But even more important reading the same materials through each viewpoint will enable everyone to better understand how others might view the same situation. this level of understanding will not only help us serve our customers better but also be better business owners and employees as well.

Part One

The Business Perspective

Introduction

If you own or manage business these days I do not have to tell you how difficult that can be. Competition is at its highest in most industries and online retailers have pushed profit margins down to close to the bare minimum for many retailers. But some of those same downsides have resulted in significant upsides as well.

Though the internet has increased competition, it has also enabled many businesses to significantly expand their sales territories and have increased access to millions more potential customers. So the bottom line just might be that businesses today have even more opportunities than at any other time in history.

But even though so much has changed over the decades, one thing has remained essentially the same. Business of all shapes and sizes need to take care of their customers or risk sending them somewhere else for their purchases. That has been a problem that has always plagued business ever since another similar store opened in their same neighborhood.

Customer service is a multi-billion dollar industry and that is because customer service is such an important part of every business that people are willing to spend the money it takes to keep their customers happy. That means investing in people and support so that customers can get what they need from their business.

The problem is that all too often mixed messages are sent and the words "customer service" are more buzz words used in signage and advertising than they are a part of the culture of the business. They say they are customer focused in order to bring customers through the front door but once they are inside, they find nothing has changed.

Other businesses feel that customer service is not all that important because they can always bring in new customers through advertising to replace those that leave. While that might be true, it is an attitude that can result in severe financial hardships to the business for reasons we will discuss in this book.

Still other businesses are hesitant to invest money into customer service because it is virtually impossible to place an accurate dollar figure on the impact of providing customer service training and the supporting infrastructure necessary to improve the overall customer experience. We will discuss that attitude and the ramifications of it in this book as well.

Throughout this book we are going to do our best to clear up a few misconceptions and give you a clear look on why customer service is so important and all the reasons why you should take customer service seriously. It is our hope that we can remove a few roadblocks and get a few more people to understand the value in creating a world-class customer experience.

The great thing is that it is not difficult or expensive to get started and once you get the ball rolling momentum and the proper attitude can sustain things. But you also need to understand that a certain culture has to be developed from the top layers of the company down to the newest employee that embraces that attitude. We will go into that in more detail as well.

But the truly great thing is that any business can do this and any business can reap the benefits of creating the best possible customer experience for every customer. This is the basis of growth and financial prosperity and once you grasp that simple concept and implement it in your business you will almost instantly see the results.

So read this book and take a lot of notes. Make the content real for you by taking what you have read and determine how you can bring that concept or action into your own company or situation. There is no medal or award given for those who finish the book in the fastest amount of time. Instead, the awards go to the people who take their time and learn the material and then actually use it.

Their reward is watching their company and business grow faster than they ever thought possible.

Why Customer Service is Important

If you noticed when you purchased this book, it is part of a 3 volume series which looks at customer service from the business perspective (this volume), the employee perspective and the customer perspective. That means we are looking at the same process and the same subject from 3 different viewpoints. Because of this, a few topics are pretty much the same and I have battled against the urge to just copy sections from one book and paste them into the other two volumes. This subject is one of those but I am not going to do a cut and paste because even though the subject is similar, there are a few different aspects to look at from the business point of view.

Unless you just started your business and you have lived alone in a monastery for a few decades, you will have noticed that business today is nothing like business was for your grandfather or even father. So much has changed and not everything has changed for the better.

But the good businesses have adapted and survived and quite a few have thrived because they did what had to be done to capitalize on those changes. The really successful companies were led by visionaries who saw those changes coming and stayed ahead of them.

If you looked back a couple of hundred years you would have noticed that businesses were primarily local enterprises that served the residents of a town and possible those in the surrounding towns as well. In those old movies about life in the old west you saw every town had one general store, one bank and one saloon / hotel. One store for everything you might need.

In those days business was easy. You sold what people wanted and they had to buy it from you. They might not have liked you or your store but they had no other options. Smart businessmen still tried to treat customer's right but it wasn't that important. I would imagine people treated other right so they wouldn't get shot for the most part! But the bottom line was that people were "captive consumers" because they had no other options. You either made it yourself, grew it yourself, or bought it in town.

But then towns got larger and you had two general stores and maybe a couple of hotels and a few saloons.

Once that happened people had a few options so businessmen had to do more for their customers in order to keep them. They had to be nicer, charge lower prices, carry better products and present a better overall experience. They either did that or their customer would go somewhere else.

This trend continued with the creation of mass transit and railroads that could bring more products to more people and more people to more places. As people began to have more flexibility they had more options. This was great for them but not so much for the businesses they frequented.

Now let's fast forward to 50 years ago.

Towns grew into cities and instead of two or three hotels there might be 15 or 20. There could be 50 stores that you could purchase clothing in and several supermarkets, countless restaurants and several sources for just about anything you wanted. Plus, if something wasn't available locally you had something called "mail order" that could bring you products from all over delivered right to your home. Competition had risen to unheard of levels compared to just a hundred years ago.

Now let's talk about today. Mail order has been replaced by something called the internet which allows people to go from store to store with a few clicks of a mouse instead of getting in the car and riving over. People can compare prices and services of 10 stores in 5 minutes instead of taking all day. Today customers have more options than ever before and to make things even worse, they know they have those options!

But at the same time, with all this added competition there also comes added opportunities as well.

Just like customers can search companies all over the world through their computers your business can reach those same customers all over the world as well. So what was once a small town economy that eventually went to regional economy that same economy is now a global economy that we can all tap into if we handle it right!

This is the exact and precise reason why customer service has developed into such a strong and vital industry. Business from all over have to compete against hundreds, sometimes thousands, or other businesses for the same customers. These customers are going to go where they get the best overall value. Not just the lowest prices but the best VALUE.

They are going to go where they get the best products, the best service, the best support and the best overall customer experience. It is no longer enough to sell something for less, you have to give the customer the entire experience or risk losing that customer to someone else. This is the business environment we need to get used to!

Some people think customer service is all about processing returns and refunds but that is really a very small segment of the customer experience.

Just about every business allows returns and processes refunds. But it is HOW they go about doing those tasks and how it treats the customer throughout those processes that makes the difference!

While I dislike having to set a negative tone in the very first chapter, I also wanted to set a reality based tone to this book. We are not going to tell you what you want to hear we are going to tell you what you NEED to hear and that is that if you want your business to grow, or if you just want your business to succeed, you MUST treat customer service very carefully.

Business is a mixture of great things and a few bad things. To concentrate on the good and ignore the bad is a sure recipe for disaster. In order to be successful you need to understand both sides. You need to embrace both the good and the bad and make both of them work for you and your business. And that is exactly what this book is going to show you how to do.

We are going to make you aware of the bad and how to turn those negatives into positives. We are going to make you aware of some of the things that can hurt your business and then show you how to capitalize on those negatives to make your business better and more attractive to your customers. That is what customer service is all about.

We are going to do all of this at a very high level so you can get the information you need about customer service in as short a period of time as possible. Then it will be up to you to act upon what you think your main problems are in your business. You can do this if you really want to if you are honest with yourself and your business. Honesty is the basis of customer service so please try and be honest about things as we move forward.

Now let's get to another negative. Why customers leave.

Why Customers Leave

Even the best run business with the most awesome products and the nicest employees are going to lose customers every year. There is no escaping it no matter how hard you try or what you might do. So the approach we need to take is not eliminating customer loss but instead minimizing it. Because that is something we can accomplish and that is how our success should be measured.

Customers will leave a business for several reasons some of which are out of the control of the business. Here are some of the reasons customers will cease doing business with a particular company:

They Move

Every year a certain percentage of your customers are going to move out of the area. They will either move because they retired, got another job, liked their new area better or for any number of reasons. You can't control it and you usually cannot influence.

The bright side is that when people leave new people come in and hopefully some of them will become future customers and offset some of the loss.

They No Longer Need the Product

Depending on the types of products and services you offer your customers might eventually outgrow the need for the products you sell. If you sell diapers, for example, you will get a few years of business from every customer for every child they have. After that they will no longer have a need for diapers and unless you sell other products that they still need, you will lose them as customers. The positive side to this is that as old customers leave new parents will become new customers if your business has a positive reputation.

The same could be said for sporting goods stores, stores that deal with products for the extremely young or very old or specialty products such as health aids that people might only need for a short period of time. If you are in any of these industries you are likely to have a higher turnover just for this reason.

Sometimes entire industries vanish because of a new technology or business model comes around. If you don't think this happens just go ahead and ask anyone who owned a video rental store in the 1980's what they are doing today.

There used to be a dozen of those stores in some large towns now you will not find anything other than a kiosk somewhere.

They Pass Away

Eventually everyone passes away and this is going to happen to every customer at some point or another. This is something you just have to accept and factor into your business model. No matter what you do you cannot make someone live forever.

They Find Someplace Better

Customers will often leave once they discover there is another business in the area that either has a better selection, better products, better service or a combination of all of those things. This can happen when you allow your competition to be better or do anything better than you do. Customers are fickle and will go where they perceive they get the most or feel the most valued.

The good part about this is that at least some of the time you can control your business and always stay on top of your market and customer base. The bad thing is sometimes when the other store is part of a huge chain and you are a small business, there is no way you can match their service or buying power.

They Have a Negative or Bad Experience.

If a customer has a bad experience with your company or a product your company sells, or even if they just don't like a single employee of yours that can open the door for them to look elsewhere. When they do look elsewhere they do so with a negative view of your business so the place often look far better in comparison. Even if they appear the same or even close they might give the new business a chance just out of anger.

While there might be other reasons that people stop doing business with a company almost all of them will fall under one of the above headings. You should also take note that the average business only has control over the last two reasons. Because of that we should concentrate our efforts on those things that are under our control and address the others in our marketing and efforts to bring new customers in.

But here is one very strong reason for being pro-active with customer service. For every customer that leaves your business because of a bad experience or because another business is deemed better, you have to bring a new customer through the doors to replace the one who left. The cost of bringing that customer through your front door can cost you as much as 10 times MORE than what it might have taken to keep that existing customer happy!

Add to that the fact that it takes more to make a new customer happy than it does to keep an old customer happy and it just makes more sense. That old customer already has a level of comfort with you and your business while the new customer has to build up that trust over time. You don't just make one purchase and fall in love with a business. It takes time after time of good experience to build confidence in a business.

I am sure you would never walk up to a customer and tell them "The store down the street has the same products and offers better service and support why don't you go there?" But that is exactly what your business is telling a customer when it gives them a poor customer experience or when it fails to resolve a problem.

The point is that customers are going to leave and there is nothing you can so to stop them. But whenever there is something you can or should do you need to do it. Otherwise you will have to spend more and more on advertising not to grow your business but just to keep it at the level that it is now. I am sure that is not the way you vision using your advertising and marketing dollars.

What Exactly is a Customer

If you ask a business owner what a customer really is, they will usually say something like "A customer is someone who purchases my products and services." After all, that is what the function of the customer is. To purchase goods or services to generate revenue and profits to sustain the business and generate profits.

But customers are other things as well. And in order to be able to serve our customers better we need to understand what our customers really are as people not just revenue generators. With that in mind, here are a few things our customers are in addition to just people who purchase our products:

People Just Like You & I

It is important to understand that our customer are people just like you and I with the same needs and desires as we probably have.

Though some of our customers might be unreasonable or difficult to deal with, we have to remember that they are people just like you and I.

People Who Need to Feel Appreciated

It is often not good enough to give a customer the product they want at the price they want. It is how you go about accomplishing this that can make all the difference in the world. Customers like to feel that their business is appreciated by the employees and the business.

They do not want to feel that they are considered burdens or distractions or annoyances. Sometimes we make customers feel this way by the way we talk to them or treat them. It might be our tone or the words we use or the manner in which we behave. But we always want to make our customers feel appreciated and valued by the business.

People with Problems that Need to Be Solved.

Whether a customer needs assistance or wants to purchase a product they have a problem that needs to be addressed. Maybe they do not know which product will solve their problem the best or maybe they are not aware of how the problem might be solved at all. Either way they come to you to have their problems solved. How well you solve their problem will determine who satisfied they are with you and your business.

People Worthy of Our Respect

Customers are also people who deserve to be treated with dignity and respect even though they might not treat us that way. But since they do represent our source of revenue and because we need that revenue to survive, we need to treat them with respect and provide them with the best customer experience possible.

We should never respond in kind to foul language or disrespectful behavior. Doing so only makes tensions rise and makes the situation worse. We should always be respectful and a calming presence in all customer situations.

People with Options

We also need to keep in mind that unless you work for the government or have a total monopoly on the products and services you sell that our customers are people that have options. When people have options, that means that they are free to go and shop wherever and whenever they please.

People with options can be more discerning and "choosy" about what they do because they are not at the mercy of a single retailer or person. So the more competition you have in your business the more careful you need to be about how you treat your customers. Because they have options and they will not be afraid to use them.

People with Freedom of Choice

Similar to the above statement, unless you have your customers under contract they can come and go as they please and they are free to seek out the best deal that gives them the most of what they want. There really is no such thing as customer loyalty anymore because many businesses are showing little to no loyalty towards the customer anymore either.

The Reason Our Businesses Exist

Have you stopped and thought about the most important thing a customer is to a business? The customer is the total reason that this business remains in business today! Without the customer there are not sales. Without any sales there is no revenue. Without revenue there is no money coming in to pay salaries and overhead let alone pay for inventory of new products to sell.

So therefore it is not an exaggeration to say that without our customers there would be no business. And without any business there would be no employees. So that in a nutshell should put the value of the customer clearly in focus for any business owner, manager or supervisor.

What Customers Want

There are certain core values that almost every customer want from the businesses they patronize. They might value one or two items more than the others but all of these will have some impact on how the customer feels about you and your business.

Here are some of the most important things a customer looks for in a business:

Honesty

Customers want to believe in the people they deal with. They want to believe that they are being told the truth and are not being deceived or lied to. They want to feel that they are being directed to a particular product because it is the best one for their needs and not because it is the product the salesman earns the largest commission for selling.

Customers sometimes feel vulnerable when they are not capable or knowledgeable enough to make the right decision on their own.

They want to be able to trust the people they are opening up to and not feel that they are being taken advantage of. In other words, they want to walk out of your store feeling confident in what they were told and the decisions they made based on that knowledge.

Honesty and trust can take a long time to build and just seconds to tear down so make sure every employee is being truthful and up front with every customer at all times. This is the only way to build a good business with a strong reputation.

Respect

Customers want to feel that they are respected. Not just by the way that the employees treat them but by the way the business is designed and run as well. That means having policies and procedures that are fair to the customer and being responsive to their needs and problems.

Friendliness

Customers want to enjoy the experience of doing business with you. They want a friendly atmosphere that makes it enjoyable to purchase your products and interact with your staff. They want a business that is willing to engage with them and provide a positive and upbeat shopping experience.

Concern

Customers often have problems and when they do they like other people and their businesses to at least show concern for their issues. This does not mean you have to accept responsibility or give them things they are not entitled to. But what it does mean is that the business and their employees should not dismiss any concerns without spending the time to listen to the customer. You must always remember that even though these problems might not seem important to you that they are important, sometimes critical to the customer.

Timeliness

Customers want things quickly. They want answers quickly and they want them when they are promised. If you say you are going to call back today, then you had better call back today even if to say that you don't have what you had promised them yet. Most customers might be disappointed but they will understand and appreciate the call.

They also do not like to wait. If they walk in and see long lines at the checkout, they might just turn and walk right back out. If it takes forever to get a salesperson they might do the exact same thing. Time is valuable to most people especially those with small children and those who work two or three jobs.

They do not want to spend an hour standing on a line for something they should be able to buy in 5 minutes. Some customers are more impatient than others so just because some people are willing to stand on line doesn't mean they all will.

Courtesy

This is an easy one that should apply to everyone not just a customer. All businesses and their employees should treat their customers in a courteous fashion. That means a nice greeting, a smile, and asking them what you can do for them today. Make this a pro-active process. By that I mean approaching the customer first and don't make them come to you.

Use the standard words like please and thankyou and refer to them by their last name and not their first name if you know it unless they are long-time customers with which you already have a relationship. Many people do not like "strangers" to refer to them by their first name so play it safe. If they ask you to use their first name that's fine but wait so you are sure.

Compassion

Similar to showing concern, customers like it when people say they are sorry that they are having this particular problem.They like it when people tell them they want to help them resolve it and will do all they can to do so.

Again, this is something we should do with all people not just customers. We should react this way to co-workers as well as it is more difficult to operate in a culture where we treat different people in different ways.

Accuracy

Even the fastest service and the best efforts will not be appreciated if the information or recommendations are wrong. Customers do not want to waste time doing something wrong or buying the wrong products based on even the most well intentioned salesperson or clerk. They want fast AND accurate answers and information!

That means training your employees to ask the right questions and to make sure every employee understands the importance of spending time listening to the customers. You do not want employees jumping to conclusions and making a wrong recommendation or decision. Every time someone gets wrong information or advice the end result is a waste of time, resources and also receives more frustration and stress as a result.

Knowledge

Nothing frustrates customers more than employees who have no idea what they are doing or that know little or nothing about the products they are there to sell. Employees who interact with customers MUST know the products inside and out. They need to know the products so they are aware of what every product can do and equally important, what they cannot do.

There is no way that a salesperson or customer service person can make the right decisions or recommendations without this knowledge. Without knowledge people have to resort to guesswork and more times than not this can cause a lot of problems.

Lack of knowledge also presents another problem for a business in that it makes the business look poorly equipped to take care of the customer. It makes the entire business look a bit amateurism in the eyes of the customer. Instead of appearing amateurish the business instead should look to establish themselves as a leader and resource in their marketplace. You want to become known as the place people go to first, not second or third, to get the products and information they need each time, every time.

Value

Of course every customer wants a great deal. Money is tight for most people these days and customers want their money to go as far as it possibly can go. But value is more than just money. It also includes other things such as delivery, support, service and the entire overall customer experience.

Value includes anything the customer perceives as having value in the sales process. If you are always able to allow people to get in and get out quickly most people will place a value on that. If you have the largest selection so the customer knows that they can always get what they want in one stop most people will place a value on that as well.

So while price is important, keep in mind that it is the overall value that is what is most important. Some companies are even able to charge higher prices on what they sell because they offer so many other benefits to their customers. This results in higher profits as well so it is a win-win for everyone.

If your business model concentrates solely on your prices being lower than everyone else then you are really going to have to sell your product at slim margins. But if you concentrate on total value instead of price you might just wind up making more profits without increasing sales.

Competitiveness

While most customers do not expect a perfect experience from any business, what they do expect is for every business to at least be competitive with each other. In other words, while it is great to be the best, you can often get away with being "among the best" in the eyes of the customer.

Customers basically want to feel that if they purchase from you they are going to get a fair deal. Not necessarily the very best but they know they are not going to be cheated.

So if every other business in town offers free delivery, you should as well to be competitive. If every other business is selling a product for $19.95 you should not be selling it at $39.95. You might sell some to unsuspecting customers but once they find out they will probably not set foot in your store again. You might be able to get away with selling that product at $21.95 and not suffer too much but always keep in mind that once a customer perceives that your business provides a lower value than other businesses you likely will have lost a customer.

In summary, customers want to be able to feel good about the products they purchased and where they purchased them from. They want and need their problems to be solved and they need them to be solved at a reasonable price.

Chances are your customer feels the same way as you do when it comes to what they want. Because we are all people we all are likely to want pretty much the same things. As you read each of these items in this chapter I am certain that you found yourself agreeing with most of them because that is what you would want as well.

So as you design and build your business, think about what your customers might like or want that you can add to your business. Think about what you might like as well when you have your "customer hat" on and chances are, those additions will be hits with your customers.

The True Value of a Customer

Good customer service doesn't have to cost money. In fact, it has been shown that customer service skills can actually save a company money in the long run. Studies have shown that it can cost 5 - 10 times more to get a new customer than it does to keep an existing one happy! Let's talk about that for a moment.

Think about what has to happen for a customer to change from another company or product to your company. Your company has to prove to that customer that you can produce a better product, or do something better than the company that person is using now. How do you do that? You accomplish this by trying to alter that person's perception of your company. Several common ways to accomplish this are:

- Hiring of sales people to go out and solicit sales

- Create media advertising to showcase your products and services.

- Get exposure for your product in trade publications.

- Create promotional campaigns to promote your products and services.

All of the above cost money. A lot of money! The sole focus of the above is to bring new customers to your company. Companies need new customers in order to grow or even stay the same. Every year, a certain percentage of existing customers will leave your company no matter what you do. Some will die, some will move out of your area, and some will no longer have a use for your products. In order for your company to remain in business, you must have a steady stream of customer to replace the one that leave.

If you lose customers due to poor service, this increase the number of new customer you must bring in. This places an enormous burden on the company. Existing customers already know what you can do for them. They already found something in your company that they like. That gives you an incredible advantage. Don't provide an excuse to send your customer to your competition. Keep your customer service satisfaction rating high. Involve your customers in your business and follow their suggestions.

Keeping your existing customers just makes good business sense. You've worked hard to get them. Now work even harder to keep them. Think of your existing customers as an army of unpaid salespeople! People that will pass on their good experiences to those that may also need the products and service your company can provide! The other side of the coin is also true. Your customers can also relay tales of unpleasant experiences, which can drive customer straight to your competition. Take care of your customer's every day and keep them on your side!

How much are your Customers Worth?

When you think about your customers, how much do you think they are worth to your company? If someone buys $100.00 worth of product from your company then that customer is worth $100.00, right? Not necessarily! That customer could be worth much more!

It is important to know the real worth of a customer because the human mind tends to react differently to things of different value. For example, if you buy something for $5.00 and it breaks two months later, you would probably throw it out and buy another one. If you purchased something for $500.00 and it broke two months later, you would have a totally different reaction. You would demand repair or replacement and would expend whatever efforts required to accomplish that.

The same would hold true for treating your customers. You would treat a customer better if they represented a larger value to the company. You may feel you treat everyone the same but the amount of business a company does with a customer is bound to influence these decisions.

The value of a customer includes the value of his or her recent purchases, recurring purchases, and the amount of business that customer represents in the future. These are concrete values. Other things that should be taken into consideration would include the customer's ability to influence other people to do business with your company, word of mouth advertising, and the industry in which the customer is involved. (Can the customer help you obtain additional business within the customers industry?)

Here's an example:

A customer walks into a deli and buys a sandwich for $4.00 and a drink for $1.00. He goes back to his office and finds the sandwich is full of poor quality meat with lots of fat in it. He goes back to the deli and demands a new sandwich. The deli owner refuses and an argument starts. The deli owner says to himself; "This guy only spent 5 bucks. This argument is just not worth my time. Let him go somewhere else." He tells the guy to leave the deli.

What did the deli owner lose? The sandwich cost him $2.00 to make so he saved $2.00. He did lose a customer but that was only $5.00 so no big deal.

Wrong! Let's look at things a different way. This customer eats lunch out twice a week. That's $10.00 per week or $520.00 per year. He also eats in an office with 20 other people that also eat out twice a week. He goes back and tells them how he was treated. Two more people decide they don't like that kind of treatment so they don't go back. That's $520 X 2 or $1020.00 more lost. So far the deli owner lost $1560.00! The customer then finds a new deli that is looking to add customers. Their sandwiches are bigger and their prices are better. It's a bit of a drive but the switch off going so that one person is making the trip. Eventually the other people in the office see the bigger and better sandwiches and 5 more people switch. That's $520 X 5 or $2600.00. The deli owner has now lost $3620.00 all because he chose to save $2.00 on replacing a sandwich! What was the value of that customer? Was it $5.00 or $3620.00? Do you think the deli owner would have treated this customer just a little bit different if he had realized this customer's true value?

You may think this is funny or just plain outrageous but it can happen. I personally know a gentleman that owned an electronic repair business. One of his major accounts was a string of video stores. One store manager made an unreasonable request and this gentleman refused to honor the request because it would mean $100.00 loss for something that was not his fault.

The store manager found someone else to do his store repairs and eventually the new business took all the stores in that chain away. It can and does happen. Don't let it happen to you!

In the case of the deli above, who knows what other business may have been lost? Maybe the owner of the company would like to have some company meetings catered. Who do you think will get that business? There are also employee businesses such as Christenings, graduations, etc. that may require catering. All this needs to be figured into the equation.

In the case of service businesses, we must figure in the cost of service contracts, maintenance contracts, equipment purchases, life span of equipment, and one more big item: supplies. Supplies are important because they represent on-going or recurring revenue. The customer may buy a machine every five years but they will buy supplies every month. In most cases the profit on supplies is where the money is made! All these things must be considered when trying to establish the true value of the customer.

The next time you are talking with a customer, place a large value on him and see if you are willing to go the extra mile for him the. I think you will be surprised how your attitude will change!

The Customer Service Chain

One common misconception when it comes to business owners is that the only people who need to be trained in customer service or know customer service techniques are the people who come in direct contact every day with the customers. This approach is not only extremely flawed but can cause serious damage to the business.

Let me explain.

The best way to describe the customer experience is by comparing it to a chain where every part of the experience is represented by a single link. So the salesperson would be a link, the checkout or cashier would be a link, the product would be a link, delivery would be a link, etc., etc. If after sale installation or set-up is included that would be another link in the chain.

The problem is that a chain is only as good or as strong as its weakest link.

So if the salesman recommends the perfect product but the delivery people show up 3 hours late with the wrong model, the entire experience fails. If the perfect product is purchased by a wonderful salesperson and cashier and it is delivered on time and installed perfectly but the billing department charges you the wrong price or your loan is at a different interest rate, the entire experience fails.

So the reality is that everyone who has any function in your company can possibly be part of the customer experience at any time. This includes people in the billing or credit department, the people who order product or maintain the warehouse, the sales force, the people who clean the parking lot, the actual customer service personnel and anyone else who has a function in the company.

If any of these individuals does something wrong, because they made a mistake or was not thinking about the customer then this can present a real problem for the business. That is why it is so important to have everyone in the company trained in customer service.

If you still have any doubts, here are ways that different departments or people in a company can either help or hinder the customer experience:

Sales

If the products you recommend to customers are not going to resolve their problems or meet their needs then that is going to cause problems. If the sales people do not ask questions, or if they do not listen to the customers as they talk, that is going to create problems. If the sales people do not make the customer feel good about doing business with your company that is going to hurt the company as well.

These might all sound like little things that can easily be remedied but the idea is to not cause the problem in the first place. Many customers will never give you a second chance no matter how good you are in resolving the problem or how sorry you tell them you are that it even happened.

Checkout (Cashiers)

If the cashier lines are really long because people are not paying attention to the lines or are aware of their importance that can create a problem. People want to get in and out fast and when they can't at your store they might go somewhere else.

If the cashiers are not pleasant or if they make mistakes in counting out change or if they run a credit through twice instead of once those can all become problems. If the cashier bags the products poorly and breaks, scratches or dents their purchase that is not likely to go over well either.

Problem Resolution

No matter how hard you try or how well intentioned you try to be, problems will still occur. But how you handle those problems can mean the difference between a lost customer and a customer for life. If you staff is not aware how to interact with angry or disgruntled customers they can make small problems worse and large problems explode.

Though everyone should be trained in customer service techniques these are the people who should be trained first because they will be able to put those skills to use faster and more often than other people. Regardless of the cost of the training the amount of time and money these skills will save you in faster and easier problem resolution will pay for that training several times over.

Billing

Imagine how you would feel if you received a bill that was twice the amount that it should be. Or if you paid in cash but still received a bill a few weeks later. Or how about financing a purchase and then getting the paperwork at double the stated interest rate?

Not only are we impacting the amount of money involved but customer often few resolving these types of problems as very stressful. Even though it might have only been a wrong keystroke or two, the effects can be severe.

People are very protective about their money and anything that threatens to take any of it away can quickly become a major problem.

As far as customer service is concerned, it is important that you have easy to access and fair policies and procedures for questions and resolving financial or payment issues. This is critical because when customers find billing or credit problems they need, not just want, to be able to resolve them as quickly as possible. The longer the problem exists the more worried and angry the customer is going to become.

Service

Even the best or fastest service is good enough if the repairs or work done is not done correctly or doesn't last! Service performed should be of the highest quality and the people that do the service must be aware of the customer's feelings and needs. This way they can more accurately choose their wording and approach to minimize any problems, misunderstanding or other issues.

Keep in mind that almost all service is considered a negative situation unless there is an upgrade involved. This is because the product either broke (negative) or that the customer has to pay for something but not get anything new for their money (slight negative). After all no one gets excited about an oil change or preventive maintenance on anything. So since the situation starts off as a negative we must take measures to turn it into a positive or at least not make it any more negative.

Warehouse

You can have the best prices and the best sales but if there is no product on the shelves to meet the demand your customers are not going to be happy. The same goes for product that you supposedly have but no one can find because the warehouse is not well organized. Or maybe the warehouse is careless in handling and moving the products and more customers get their purchases home only to find them dented, broken, scratched or otherwise damaged.

Do not think that the folks in the warehouse are removed from the customer experience because they are not. They need to be aware of the repercussions of their actions on the customer and their experience. Then they might become a little bit more careful or become better organized. Every little bit helps and these actions could make a huge impact on your customers.

The other thing to think about is that getting a product is good shape without any damage is something people usually take for granted. So you are not going to get a pat on the back for giving someone a product that is not damaged. But that same person will be quick to complain when they get something damaged in any way.

Delivery

Imagine you are excited to get that brand new 155 inch flat screen TV that you have been saving up for. The delivery men said they will be there at 10AM but it's now 4PM and no one has called. You can't get a hold of anyone either and have left a few messages. Finally they show up at 6:30 and bring in the TV and at the same time track muddy footprints all over your brand new snow white carpeting. Plus, they scratched the molding on your door frames as well. When you asked them why they were so late, you got an attitude in return.

Many businesses do not really understand just how much their delivery people and service can impact the customer experience. This is especially true when delivery is free. When that is the case businesses sometimes feel that if a customer isn't paying for something then they shouldn't complain if it isn't perfect.

But here is something to really sit down and think about: The delivery process is often the last part of the sales process and what the customer is going to be left with memories about. If that part of the process is bad, they are likely to forget about the great price and the helpful salesperson. All they are going to remember is the long wait and the hours it took to clean the mud out of the carpets.

Maintenance

It should be no purpose that customers like to see clean and well maintained stores.

If your parking lot looks like a tornado just went through and your rest rooms look like they haven't seen a cleaning in 5 years, your customers are going to develop a negative perception of your entire organization. Not just the store but of your entire organization.

Outward appearance is a direct reflection on how the business is run and how it views their customers. The idea is that if a business doesn't care enough about the customer to provide a clean environment for them to shop in, then the rest of the business is not likely to care about them either.

Your maintenance staff has to care about the appearance of the store and understand how it factors in with what the customer thinks about the entire business. They need to see the connection and they need to understand why it is so important to keep things looking nice and functioning properly. This means doing frequent inspections and taking care of things before they get noticed by the customer. And if they are noticed by the customer they need to be addressed immediately after they are reported.

Management

One might think that the owner of the company, who may or may not be actively involved in the day to day operations of the business, might not be involved in customer service.

If you are one who feels that way, prepare to have that view challenged.

In some ways the management and ownership of the company are responsible for customer service at its most important point. That point is the direction which the company wants taken as far as treatment of customers is concerned.

Owners and management MUST provide a unified message that clearly shows the direction the employees are to take when it comes to taking care of the customer. But even more important, ownership and management MUST follow that same direction and act in the same manner and show themselves as examples of how people should be acting.

For example, if you tell employees to be very liberal with your return policy then you cannot go to employees and yell at them or berate them for doing so. You cannot tell employees to give customers more and then turn around and yell at them for using more resources! Though this might sound a bit silly, this type of behavior is quite common in many companies today. You cannot support the true direction of the company by creating a "Do as I say not as I Do" mentality.

As you can see, almost everyone, if not everyone, in the company can have a significant impact, both positive and negative impact on customer service. We cannot just train a few people involved in direct customer contact and feel that this is enough. While it might be a good start we are still placing the rest of the customer experience at risk.

Since the customer experience is like a chain, any weak link can cause the entire chain to fail. Once this happens we dramatically increase the possibility of a customer leaving to go over to the competition. Once this happen it can be extremely difficult to get them back again.

Even if they don't leave you are still going to have to work on restoring their faith in your business. Since it can take as many as 10 positive experiences to override the effects of just one negative experience, you want to do everything in your power to eliminate as many of those negative experiences as possible.

Exceeding Expectations

Everyone understands that our customers have certain expectations. If we want our customers to keep buying from us, we have to meet those expectations. But the fact is, if we give our customers what they expect it probably isn't going to be enough. If we want to create loyal and satisfied customers we are going to have to exceed their expectations.

People are unique individuals. We think sometimes in strange ways and react in even stranger ways. One of those ways is that whenever we get something we expect, we are not impressed or really satisfied. We just got what we expected so no big deal. So it's not like we are going to get any "points" for just giving someone what they thought they were going to get.

We have to give them more.

If everyone in town is selling a product for $229.95 with free delivery and set-up, offering to sell that product for the same price with free delivery is not going to impress anyone.

People would probably just buy it from whatever store was closest or the most convenient. You are not going to get any word of mouth advertising from that. But if you added a free accessory or lowered the price or included something else of value for the same price that might make a difference.

If everyone else is offering a 60 day return policy and you offer a 30 day policy that is not good in the eyes of most customers. But if you offered a 90-day return policy, that might make people take notice. It's not likely to cost you much money to do so but it makes your business look better.

We could go on and on and site example after example but the bottom line is that you not only have to meet what everyone else is offering but you often have to beat it in order to keep existing customers and bring in new ones. We should be aiming to meet the status quo, we should be looking to beat it and become known as the best of the best.

It is amazing how people who supposedly are intelligent enough to rise up the ranks at major businesses fail to grasp this extremely basic and simple concept. I was at a meeting once where someone from a very large and well-known and respected company was talking about customer service and product quality.

It was at this meeting that I heard this upper manager make a statement that I thought I misheard. But he actually said it.

When someone made a statement that customer satisfaction had gone down because product quality went down over the last year, that person was told that he was not doing his job because he did not "reset the customer's expectations."

Yes, that is exactly what he said. His stance was that if you cannot meet the expectations of the customer then it was up to you to reset those expectations to a level that you could meet! There are no words to adequately describe the utter stupidity and cluelessness that this statement had made!

Customers expect what they expect because that is what they are used to receiving from other companies or how they were used to being treated in the past. They don't pick up expectations out of thin air. They have those expectations because that is what they are used to. You cannot "reset" those expectations just because you can't or are unwilling to achieve them!

Are some expectations way over the top even bordering on being ridiculous? Of course they are. Some customers think that they are entitled to the world or whatever they want whenever they want it. But I am not talking about those customers. I am talking about the expectations of those customers who are based in reality and are reasonable. Those are the people we have to impress the heck out of if we want to keep them coming back again and again.

But this requires a certain type of attitude and that attitude starts at the top and is brought down to every employee in every department. It is an attitude that the customer comes first and that we should be looking for ways to give the customer as much as we reasonably can. We send the message that we should be looking to exceed what the customer expects and not trying to give them as little as we can and still get by.

Which brings us to the next topic which is how we can give the customer more of what they want while still behaving in a responsible manner that protects the business as well.

The Needs of Both the Customer & the Business

It would be easy to give every customer exactly what they were looking for and to also throw in a few more things for good measure. That would make the customer happy and they would soon be telling their family and friends about the great deals they got and the great treatment they had received. Your business would be the talk of the town and people would flock to your doors.

But one day those customers would find those doors locked because you would be out of business. The fact is that every business, no matter how customer focused and committed it might be, need to protect its own interests as well as the interests of the customer. It is a kind of balancing act that we have to go through every single week.

There are two things we need to consider before we go any further. First, the customer doesn't really care one way or another about the needs of your business or anyone else's. All they care about is getting what they want when they want it. So, trying to explain this to them is likely not going to go over well.

But the second thing is that if we do not protect the interests of the business as well as the interests of the customer the business is not likely to survive for the long-term. So the result is going to be that the business will cease to exist at some point. What that means is that the business is not going to be around at all when the customers do need it. So even though they customer doesn't care about the health of the business they really should.

What all this means is that there has to be a limit in what we offer the customer as far as value and problem resolution is concerned. But we should still make every effort to be fair and still try to give as much as we can responsibly afford. We should not use the "health of the business" as an excuse for giving the customers as little as possible.

There are several factors that go into what we can and should offer a customer as far as a resolution or settlement. Here are a few of the most common factors we should consider:

The Value of the Customer to the Business

Though many customers will not agree and feel that this is not fair and that everyone should be treated equally, the reality of the situation is that you are going to treat a very big customer at a different level than you are the one-time buyer who only spent $5 in your store. This is just common sense. You always need to make sure to factor in the particular customer and his or her value to your business whenever you are making a decision on what is appropriate.

Legal Requirements

This is one area where we might have little leeway or choice. If there are certain laws or statues that guarantee your customer certain rights or protection under the law then we have to uphold those requirements. For example, we cannot refuse to honor a warranty or adhere to a publicized return policy without a legal and good reason.

But these laws or statues are usually considered minimum protection for the customer. So while we cannot do anything less we often are able to go above and beyond and do more. But since we are not lawyers, we urge you to contact your company lawyer to determine what your exposure and obligations are under the law.

The Scope or Severity of the Problem

We should also take into consideration the severity of the particular situation or problem when determining a resolution. Particularly difficult or severe problems or issues usually require a more costly or involved resolution.

For example, if you sold a homeowner a kitchen faucet and it stopped working a week after the guarantee was over you might refuse to replace it citing the warranty or direct them to the manufacturer. That is within your obligation since the warranty was over.

But if the faucet failed and leaked all over and damaged her cabinets and floor and basement, you might want to at least offer her a free replacement as a good faith gesture. You wouldn't be admitting guilt or responsibility but would be seen as trying to make things a bit easier with a customer who has far greater issues to deal with. In other words, you would be seen as trying to do the right thing for the customer.

The Specific Situation

Just like no two people are alike no two situations are alike either. So what we offer one customer might not be appropriate for another. So we need to take each situation and customer up separately and do what we think is proper for that customer at this time.

Setting of Precedents

Sometimes doing the right thing can get you into trouble. Under the law we cannot treat people differently based on age, sex, nationality and other items. While this doesn't mean we do not have the flexibility to do certain things for some customers, we need to consider what might happen if this customer were to tell others about what they got. The result might be other customers coming forward and demanding the same settlement or resolution as the others got.

The problem is that while we might feel sorry for someone such as the elderly who might not have the ability to resolve the problem on their own, that others might say you cannot favor one age group or other group over another and they would be right. There will always be those customers who will not care about anything except getting the most from you as they can whether or not they are actually entitled to it.

The bottom line is that management must put into place a system where employees are encouraged to give the customers fair treatment and as much of what they need as possible within certain limits. How we go about this can be tricky. We might require management approval or create a set of guideline which an employee can work within.

We are going to get into that now.

Rules, Policies & Procedures

If you own a company with more than 2 employees, you are going to have several minds each thinking and acting independently and this can cause serious problems when it comes to customer service. That is because there will be one thing missing from your company that almost every customer needs from your business.

That is continuity or service.

What that means is that customer want to make reasonably certain that they are going to receive the same responses and same level of service regardless of who they talk to. If your company has more than one branch office then this becomes even more critical. In those cases you want your customers to feel sure that they will receive the same level of treatment no matter what location they go to.

If you look at the franchise business model you will see that there are strict rules, policies and procedures put in place for every aspect of the business. They don't do these things to make life more difficult on the employees. The do it to make sure the same experience is felt in all locations.

This is important because when it comes to franchises with many locations customer want to know that they will get the same burger in Florida that they are getting at home in Maine. Or that they will get the same quality carpet cleaning in Florida that they used to get in Maine. Regardless of the food or product involved, it is the continuity of the experience and product that matters most.

The same occurs with employees as well. If one or two employees treat customers better than all the others customers are going to all ask for those one or two employees and try to stay away from everyone else. That will disrupt service and effect wait times and other things as well. To avoid this, we need to establish rules that help guide and determine who customers are treated within the business.

We do this by establishing rules and creating policies and procedures that will give employees a certain set of parameters within which they can make decisions. This not only helps insure a similar experience throughout the company but it also speeds up the process as well.

For example, let's say we develop a policy that says that any employee can make an immediate decision as long as the cost to the company is less than $50. What they will enable is for an employee to resolve a problem right there on the spot without having to slow things down by getting a manager or supervisor approval. The result is the customer gets a resolution right away so they do not have the chance to think about it for a while and get more upset. Also, more customer get to be helped in the same amount of time which makes it easier on everyone in the long run.

But it accomplishes all of this in such a manner that the interests and financial health of the company is preserved and protected as well. More expensive solutions are not banned but rather just require management approval. The vast majority of the resolutions, those under the $50 or other approved levels, just quickly go through the process.

In order to create an effective and customer friendly policy or procedure there are a few things we should consider. While there may be times that other factors will come into play, here are a few of the major things that should be considered whenever a new policy or procedure is designed and implemented:

It Should Be Fair

Whenever you institute any policy or procedure, or whenever you evaluate a current one, you must make sure that it is fair to both the customer and the company. If it is overly restrictive or favors the company too much the customer will see right through the real reason for having that policy in place.

Look at every policy and procedure and make sure that it is not too one-sided and favors either party too much. If something is perceived fair by the customer then you stand a much better chance of getting the customer to accept the policy and not fight it. Plus, if the situation should take a legal turn, a fair policy can be good for the business as it will show a good faith effort to resolve the situation.

It Should Be Legal

All policies and procedures must align with existing laws and customer rights. You cannot arbitrarily create any policy or procedure that removes the rights from any customer without a really good and legal reason.

It Should be Streamlined

Bulky and convoluted policies and procedures just take too much time to go through and can become far too confusing for both the employees and the customers.

Your policies should be straight forward, easy to understand, easy to implement and just make sense to everyone involved. When creating a new policy or procedure create it and then look for ways to make it easier. There are always ways to make things easier. We just have to look for them.

It Should Address a Real Issue

Policies and procedures should address real and current issues. If you have rules and procedures that address issues that no longer exist, it might be time to get rid of them. The more rules and policies an employee has to remember the more likely they are going to forget some of them. Keep them current, keep them short and make sure they fulfill their intended purpose.

It Should Make Things Easier NOT More Complicated

The reason many employees hate policies and procedures is that they make it harder to resolve problems or to get certain things done. The more difficult or cumbersome something is the less likely it is that employees will use it. Instead they will try to find easier ways of accomplishing the same thing. That will lead to different responses by different employees and create more confusion instead of less. So design your policies and procedures to make the employee's jobs easier not harder.

It Should Address Both the Customer's Needs & the Needs of the Business

We mentioned that the policies have to be fair for both sides and that also means that they need to address the needs of both sides as well. There should be give and take built into the policy so that both the business and the customer get at least some of what they both need.

In this case it would be giving the customers more while still protecting the assets and the long term financial health of the business. Any policy that is too one-sided in either direction is not good for the business.

As you design your policies and procedures make every effort to make them easy to understand and even easier to implement. Having policies in place that allow all employees to perform at a similar or more structured manner helps you provide a constant level of customer service and treatment from employee to employee and also from location to location.

This should be the ultimate goal of every policy and procedure. If something doesn't help achieve that goal or protect the business or the customer then it should be questioned as to whether it is really needed in the first place.

Resolving Problems

When you think of customer service, you think of problems, refunds and advice. Refunds and advice usually are no problem and just take a bit of time and research to resolve most situations. But when problems occur, these are the times we can either make the company shine or cause problems to worsen over time.

Whenever a customer has a problem there are a few things that they want to see or experience. Though these are just some of the most popular things a customer looks for they will make an excellent starting point for any customer service department.

When customers have a problem they want to see:

Concern

People want to see that other people are taking their problem seriously and are at least willing to listen to the problem before making a decision.

This means having people who are aware of this and who will spend time listening to the customer and making sure they feel like they want to help resolve the situation.

This is one of the reasons why people in this capacity really need customer service training so they not only understand the problem but the customer as well. Sometimes knowing the techniques will make all the difference as the individual can say all the right things at the right time and make the situation better not worse.

Empathy

Similar to concern, they like to hear someone say that they are sorry the customer has been placed in this situation. This does not mean we have to admit guilt or even accept responsibility for the problem however. But we should let the customer know we feel bad that they have to go through this. This will have a calming effect on the customer.

This is one of the cornerstones of customer service and why people need these skills. Since everything we do should be designed to move the customer to a happier or less negative frame of mind, knowing what to say and why it needs to be said is critical in properly handling these situations.

Fairness

Though you might not believe it, the vast majority of customer just want to feel that they are being treated fairly. They don't have to get everything they want as long as they believe they were treated fairly. You can make them feel this way by treating them in a fair and equitable manner. Engage in open and honest negotiations and honestly try to help them. This is all that most customers want and expect from any business.

Speed

The thing about problems is that the longer they stay as problems the more serious they become. This is because the longer people have to think about something the larger and more important that issue becomes. What was once a little nagging problem can soon turn into a raging nightmare if left unresolved for a long enough period of time.

The longer it takes to contact the customer and provide a resolution the more expensive it is likely to be to make the issue go away. That is why every minute we spend getting an approval or researching or delaying resolution for any period of time needs to be minimized or even eliminated. When employees are empowered to make decisions on the spot the average cost of resolving a problem goes down significantly.

Conversely when employees have to go through hoops and navigate cumbersome policies the cost of resolving problems goes up considerably.

Because of this, create and structure your customer service department to be as fast and efficient as possible. It might cost a bit more to build a department in that way but you will save money I the long run and have much higher customer satisfaction.

Accuracy

Whatever is going to happen in the situation make sure it is accurate. If you make a comment or a commitment to a customer make sure you stand by it even if it costs the business money. Credibility is everything so stand by your word and everything you say.

Because of this you should think twice before you speak and never make a statement that you do not know is 100% true. Spending a few moments confirming information now can save you a lot of time, headaches and money later on. Remember your ultimate success and failure often hinges on your credibility.

Resolution

When everything is said and done, the final resolution or final answer is going to determine whether the customer is happy or not. If you handle the situation correctly and do whatever you can to make the customer happy you should be able to make the majority of customers happy.

There will always be a few that will continue to be unhappy no matter what you do so do not demand or expect 100% success. That is something to shoot for but not expect.

Always go for the win-win resolution and direct all your effort to that end goal. When your employees have that mindset almost everything will move in the right direction and customer satisfaction should get higher and higher. It is when we try to satisfy a customer by giving up as little as possible that troubles begin.

If done correctly you can take an angry customer and turn them into a customer for life. This might sound like a cliché but it is the truth. In many cases problems are a way for us to show the customer just how good we really are. Anyone can sell a customer a product but only a really great company will stand up and help them resolve a problem.

Don't let any opportunity to show a customer just how good you are. There is no better way to impress a customer than to help them resolve a problem when others wouldn't or couldn't be bothered. It is an opportunity that doesn't show up all that often so you should take advantage of it whenever you can.

Perception vs. Reality

Many businesses fall short of their goal because they do not pay attention to the way that a lot of their customers feel about them and their business. They hide behind studies and numbers and other things instead of listening or paying attention to what their customers are saying. They do not understand that not only do they have to pay attention to the reality of the situation but also to perceptions as well.

I will agree with anyone that it is not fair that perceptions need to be addressed as strongly as reality but that is still the case. The reason for this is that when someone perceives something to be a certain way that becomes their reality until proven otherwise. So in those situation perception is the same as reality so we need to adjust our thinking.

For example, if your checkout lines are pretty much standard for your industry or type of business that might tell you that this is not an issue. But if your lines are perceived to be too long that can be a problem because that perception might keep customers away from your store.

It makes no difference that your customers think your lines are too long because they happened to come in 3 times when people called in sick or when you had especially high sales days. That makes no difference. All the customer knows is that when they walked in the lines were too long. So a perception is created and will remain until they experience something different.

For this reason it is very important to have some method in place to gather feedback from your customers. This might be a survey or a questionnaire or even someone asking people as they leave the store how their experience was.

You are always going to get people who will look for things to complain about or criticize so there is no need to act on every comment or every complaint. But if the same complaints or comments are made many times, this is something you should look into. Because if several people feel the same way chances are that others are also going to feel that way.

Some business owner's feel that if their business is working well in their eyes that this should be good enough. While this might be true because the business owner and management hopefully is skilled in building a business, the end result is that it really doesn't matter what management thinks. Management doesn't buy products, the customers do.

So from this point on, listen to your customers. Ask them questions and then listen to the answers. Catalog the answers and look for similarities. Always look for ways to make things better. Very often complaints will point you to things you thought were running just fine. But improvement are always possible and whenever you can make something better you should.

Also keep in mind that your competition is also looking for ways to make their businesses better as well. That means they are going to keep improving thing in their business so that they can be the best at what they sell and do. So you must do the same. It is not what you think that matters. Your customer does not choose where to by based on how you feel about your business.

They buy based on their perception and their experiences. It is time you listened to how your customers feel whether those feelings are accurate or not. If they are accurate listen to them and act upon them to make improvement. If they are not accurate figure out what you can do to wipe out that false impression and replace it with a few positive ones. That is exactly how great businesses and loyal customers are created.

Sending the Right Message

When it comes to how employees treat your customers and handle their problems and requests, they take their lead and direction from the management of the company. In other words, they should be doing as they are told to do. This means that the direction of the company must be coming from the ownership or management.

This message is delivered in two ways.

First, it is delivered through the policies and procedures that are designed and put in place by management. These let the employees how the parameters within which they are to work and make decisions. They also give a clear message on how things should be done in the most common situations.

Second, the message is delivered through the behavior and actions of management and ownership.

In other words, management and ownership should be behaving in a manner consistent with the message they wish to send. As far as customer service is concerned, they should be following the same rules and procedures and approach as they expect the employees to follow.

The reality is that both of the ways ownership and management deliver the message are closely tied to each other. The policies and procedures need to closely align with the behavior of the people using them and enforcing them. If the people enforcing them routinely disregard them or do not follow them, this sends a confusing and wrong message to everyone else.

This does not mean that management cannot bend the rules or make exceptions to the rules because sometimes that is the right thing to do. But when this happens it is often good to explain why something was done differently in that particular situation. This is not because management has to account for themselves or explain themselves to the employees. It is done so people still believe that everyone is enforcing and following the rules like they are expected to do.

In order to be successful every business needs to have a consistent message when it comes to how to treat customers. That message also needs to be taken down to how the company treats the employees as well. After all you cannot expect employees who are yelled at and berated on a consistent basis to treat customers with dignity and respect.

Customer care has got to be part of the culture of the company. A culture where everyone is treated well and with respect. We have to make sure that we make employees aware that everyone, both customers and employees must be treated with respect at all times. That means not only treating customers well but each other as well.

This is one of those messages that has to be delivered from the top down. It cannot work any other way. We run the company in a certain manner and we show employees how to treat customers by setting the proper example ourselves. This is the only way this system can function properly. It must come from the top down every day and every hour of the day.

Providing Training

It never ceases to amaze me that companies have no problem training their salesmen on products and their service technicians on how to service the products they sell but stop short of training their employees on how to treat customers and each other. For some reason I guess known only to the people who make these decisions, they figure that employees should just know these things as a matter of living their lives. I guess they figure it is just like breathing. Everyone knows how to do it.

But the problem is that we all don't know how to do it. We might have our own ideas and opinions as to how it's done but those opinions might be 100% wrong. We all are a product of our upbringing and the atmosphere in which we are raised. That may or may not have prepared us for knowing how to interact with other people.

But even if our upbringing and social skills are pretty good there is still another problem that needs to be addressed. We all cannot do our jobs according to our own interpretation of how people should be treated.

We cannot have 50 people doing the same thing 50 different ways and expect to get anywhere close to a unified method of doing business. Instead we have confusion between each other and within our customer base. That is simply not acceptable if you want to have a well operating company that is poised for growth and success.

The common misconception is that training just teaches us why we need to do certain things. While that is a crucial aspect of training the other part of training, sometimes even more important, is showing us HOW to do those things and how to do them in the right way. One of the most beneficial aspects of training within a company is that it shows everyone how to do the same things in the same way.

Training, when done properly will show everyone the right way to do their jobs, interact with others and help the company develop a unified method of doing business and providing service to their customers. So instead of having one task done 50 different ways we can have 50 tasks all done pretty much the same way.

The result is customer A getting the same experience and treatment as customer M even though they saw two different employees in two different locations.

It also means employee A delivering the same message as employee Y even though they are in different offices or departments. So more than just providing knowledge and insight training also gives everyone the same direction so we all can function as one unit instead of individuals.

Some business complain that they cannot provide training in customer service to every employee because of the costs involved. But I have a different view on that because I look at things in different ways. In my opinion customer service training doesn't cost a company money at all. In fact, providing good training to every employee will actually save the company money in the long run!

Though it would be ideal if everyone in the company received comprehensive training in all aspects of customer service sometimes that is not practical or even possible. If that is the case with your company, consider a multi-level approach to training where some receive comprehensive training up-front while other receive their training either in stages or by department.

For example, you might provide full or comprehensive training to everyone in the customer service department because their everyday job requires direct and personal interaction with customers. So training there would provide immediate benefit to the business. In other words, you would get the most for your training dollar by training these individuals or departments first.

If possible you might include your sales force in the first group as well or they should be in the second group along with other direct contact people such as cashiers or other personnel. Next would come delivery people and finance people and service people if you offer service to your customers. Finally, back office people, or other people who do not have day to day direct customer contact would receive their training.

With this approach eventually over time everyone would receive their training. The advantage of this approach is that it will cost less money upfront and the expenses can be absorbed over a longer period of time. The disadvantage is that it will take longer for everyone to get trained and during that time customers might receive less than optimal treatment.

Another approach might be to give everyone training in stages where different topics or classes would be given to everyone at pretty much the same time and everyone would receive several classes or training sessions over a longer period of time.

For example everyone might receive basic customer service techniques and listening techniques first followed by problem solving and conflict resolution training at a later date. The advantages to this approach is that everyone would receive training at the same time so everyone can be on the same page as training progresses.

The customers would all benefit from day one as everyone would receive basic training first. The disadvantages of this approach is that advanced topics would come later so customers might not receive the best overall experience when they have problems. But you might also deal with that by training all the people just in the customer service department in all aspects of customer service all at once while everyone else gets their training in stages.

Types of Training

There are several ways to bring training to all your employees. Here are a few of the most common sources of training along with their advantages and potential disadvantages:

Seminars

These classes are given by outside companies and are usually scheduled somewhere in your area. They are either basic or advanced and are given in a group format. They are usually held in local hotels or other conferences centers. The advantages are that they are held somewhat locally so travel time is limited. If everyone takes the same classes then everyone will get pretty much the same training as well. The disadvantages are that they are somewhat expensive especially when you have a lot of people to be trained and they require people to take off of work to get trained.

College Classes

These are classes held in local schools or colleges and they are in a group setting as well. These are less expensive at time which can be an advantage but they are usually longer in length which means employees will have to take off more time in order to complete training.

In-House Training

If you have a lot of employees to train this might be an attractive option for you. You can hire a trainer to develop a training program specific to your business and your need and present it in-house. This will allow easier access to employees and require less time off from work in order to get training. Increase ease will always help insure that everyone actually gets the training. Targeted content is more beneficial as well.

As far as costs are concerned that will depend on the amount of training and the number of employees that are to be trained. This option could be cheaper than seminars and targeted content would make the training more specific and useful.

Self-Administered Training

This is where you make every individual responsible for their own training.

This is not the best method for several reasons. First of all, not everyone will comply. Second, many people will take the easiest or quickest option to get training done and the quality might be lacking. Third, with everyone taking different training there will be no standards in place for how things are done and how every person thinks. This is the least desirable option for these reasons and probably a few more as well.

Books or Videos

Having people read books and watch videos is an interesting choice and might be one way to get people trained quickly and inexpensively. You can find books or videos that you feel provide adequate training and then purchase licenses or copies of the books for every employee. You can then give them time off during their workday to read the books or watch the videos. This is a better alternative than expecting them to do it on their own time because this will insure that they actually take the training or read the books.

Compliance can be an issue as you are not going to know which employees will actually do the work and which will just say they did. For this reason I think it is a good idea to hold a few group sessions where people can discuss the training they just took and compare ideas. This accomplishes a few different things. First it makes people read the materials because they will see the group sessions as a kind of test to see if they took the training.

Second, the exchange of thoughts and ideas will help people understand and get different views on what they read. This is one of the most important aspects of a seminar training format.

Which is Best?

If you can afford it the in-house model is the best because it allows you to control more of the training format and content. Second it makes taking the training easier and if sessions are short enough people can take them during their workday without taking time off. This will increase productivity and require less back-up scheduling to cover missing employees out taking training or attending seminars.

If you have someone on staff that is a trainer or can become a trainer this can make it far more cost effective as well. Plus, an added benefit is that as new employees come into the company they can be easily trained as well without having to wait for the next round of seminars to come to town.

You can even combine in-house training with books and videos to minimize the session time thus making it faster and easier to attend and complete the training.

Whatever you decide, just make sure that everyone receives the training they need to do their jobs in the best manner possible. Not only will your company run smoother and more efficiently but it will also help raise customer satisfaction as it reduces stress and raises productivity as well.

Conclusion

At this point we hope we convinced you that customer service should be an integral part of your business. Not just because of customer satisfaction and resolving customer problems but because it will help make your business stronger, more successful and help position it for better growth as well. If we have convinced you that, that's great! If we somehow have not convinced you, we hope you will read this book again and give it another shot.

At this point in time when competition is so fierce and with so many people looking to go after your customers and take them away from you, it just makes sense to do whatever it takes to keep your customers in your business. Plus, it makes sense that you should also want to position yourself to take away other businesses customer as well. In other words, if you don't do it to them they are going to do it to you. Be prepared to deal with that either now or later.

We are at a point in this economy where businesses that are properly positioned and prepared to take advantage of opportunities are going to be richly rewarded. The good news is that there are a lot of poorly run businesses out there just waiting to have their customers taken away from them because they were either too lazy or too clueless to realize what they were doing. The bad news is that your company might be one of them. Since you are reading this book I doubt that is the case but you never know.

The other piece of good news is that it is usually never too late to straighten things out and become a customer focused business moving forward. It is going to take time to change perceptions and get people to come back to you but it can be done. Don't let anyone tell you it can't. If you are willing and patient, it can be done.

If you are one of those business owners who have to see everything in black and white and see cost/benefit analysis and everything else before you will spend a dime on training, please change that mindset. No one can tell you to the dollar how much bad service is costing you because there are so many unknowns that you just cannot measure. But I will tell you this. Whatever you think you might be losing, double or triple that figure and you probably still are underestimating things.

That is because customers are getting more and more demanding every single day and because of social media and other forms of information sharing they are becoming more and more vocal and outspoken as well. Do not give any customer a legitimate reason to speak out against your business. Do everything you possibly can to make each and every customer happy.

Make that your passion and make it your company's passion as well. Take that message and bring it to your employees. Make them understand the importance of customer service through your message and your actions. Drive that home by providing them with the training they need to carry out your instructions and provide the very best customer experience to each and every customer.

Also remember that sometimes you only get one chance to make an impression on a customer. If you fail to make a great impression you might never get a second chance. Many customers will just walk away never to return and they will not even let you know why they left! So do your very best and listen to your customers. Hear what they are saying and give your employees the tools they need to do their jobs.

Once you do that you will find things going much smoother, your employees and your customers will be much happier and there will be much less stress for everyone. If that is not the ultimate win-win resolution I am not sure what is!

Part Two

Customer Service
All You Have to Know

Employee Edition

By
David Peters

Disclaimer

Every customer and situation is different so therefore it is impossible to create one universal approach that will work in any situation. Therefore it is the responsibility of the reader to determine which parts of this book, if any, are appropriate for use in any given situation and with any given individual. The writers, publishers and resellers of this book assume no responsibility for the use or application of any or all parts of this book.

Introduction

Customer Service is an important part of business these days. Significant amounts of money are spent by almost every company these days to improve customer care and make customers happy. Some of the things companies do, like reducing waiting time and creating more generous customer service policies are obvious. But sometimes it is the things we don't see that provide the greatest benefit.

If you are reading this book chances are it was given to you by an employer or manager or you have an interest in Customer Service and wish to apply the knowledge in your career. Regardless of the reason you are reading this book, we congratulate you for wanting to learn more about customer service.

When we talk about customer service we are talking about more than someone sitting behind a desk asking you if you want a refund or an exchange. That is just the part of the process we usually equate to the term customer service. But the reality is the term customer service covers a wealth of activities and resources. All of which are combined to produce the best customer service experience possible.

One of the remarkable thing about customer service is that there are no "small" jobs. Every aspect of the customer experience is important and anyone who touches any part of that experience is important. I prefer to think about the customer service experience as a chain where every part of the experience and every person that is involved is a link in that chain. In this configuration the entire process is only as strong as its weakest link.

So wherever you might be in the experience and whatever your responsibilities or tasks might be, let me tell you right now that you are an important part of the customer service process. Your attitude and performance can make or break the entire customer experience. You be responsible for losing a customer or gaining a customer for life. It all depends on the process.

By hiring you, the company is putting its faith in you to treat your customers fairly and with a smile on your face. The company is making you part of the face of the company. It is investing its future on your efforts. That is a lot of responsibility but it can be very rewarding at the same time.

Throughout my 40 years experience in customer service I have seen single individuals make enormous improvement in customer service and profits by just doing a few little things right. I have seen people take an angry customer and calm them down and turn them into life-long happy customers. Not through magic or deception but by just treating the customer properly at all times.

This isn't difficult and it certainly isn't rocket science but there are a few things you need to know and this book is going to give you those things on a silver platter. All you need to do is use the techniques, apply the materials and your potential can be unlimited. The best thing is that once you finish the book, and even before you finish it, you can start making a difference immediately! That means you can start improving the customer experience and creating strong and vibrant customer relationships today!

As you go through this book read each chapter carefully even if you don't think it is relevant to you. The book is not long and it will not take you much time to read it all the way through. So invest the time and take your time to make it relevant to you. As you finish a chapter close the book and think about what you have read.

Think about how you can use and apply that concept or technique in your own situation. Make it real for you. Once you do that you will remember it better and longer and you will become more efficient and productive immediately.

This book may be small but it packs in a lot of information. We know your time is limited and valuable to you so we want to give you what you need as easily and quickly as possible. So let's turn the page and get started learning "all you have to know" about customer service.

Why Customer Service is Important

Perhaps the most important thing to understand as we move into learning about customer service is why it is so important to every business in existence today. After all, no business is going to hire employees and spend money on something that is not going to have a positive impact on their business. So let's see why customer service is so critical to every business today.

A few hundred years ago when towns were small and there were just a few businesses, you could treat customers any way you wanted. If you were the only general store people had to buy their food from you because there was no one else. The same for the only hotel, the only blacksmith and the only saloon/hotel. When there is only one of something, they can pretty much do what they want and treat people however they want.

But then over the years, one business in town became two then three then for and even more. People began to have options and when people have options, they do whatever is best for them. If they get a better deal or better treatment somewhere else, that's is where they are going to go. The base of power has shifted from the business over to the customers.

So unless you are the sole source for whatever product or service you sell, you are going to have to treat your customers right or they will go somewhere else. Even more important you have to treat them right according to the customers definition of right not your own. Because if people don't get what they want when they want, they will look elsewhere until they find it. While there is such a thing as customer loyalty it is significantly overrated and it grows less and less of a factor as time goes on.

Now fast forward to today and you can see a dramatic change over the last 10 or 15 years with the growth of the internet. It used to be that businesses had to worry about the competition in their town or perhaps a neighboring town as well. So a hardware store, for example, might have had to compete with 3 or 4 other hardware stores in town and perhaps 2 or 3 more in the next town over. That was probably manageable for a good businessman.

But now with the internet not only does his business have to compete with the local stores but also every hardware store on the internet as well as the big online retailers that sell just about anything that is manufactured. To make things worse, they probably sell the products for less as well because they have less overall overhead.

By now I hope you understand just how much stiffer the competition is than it used to be and how difficult it can be for any business to survive. More competition means more options which usually translates into lower prices and reduced profits as well. So most businesses now have to sell more just to keep the same revenue coming in.

Now I am not trying to depress anyone here or paint an extremely negative picture. I am just giving you a much needed dose of reality for those who might not understand just what the average business is up against these days. Sure there is bad news but there is also some very good news as well. Just as more businesses can compete with you over the internet that also means that your business can also compete with more people as well. So you have more competition but a wider and larger audience.

But customers are expensive to bring in through the doors. Advertising isn't cheap and businesses often spend a ton of money getting new people to walk through their doors each and every day. They need to do this because every business loses a certain percentage of their customers every year even when it does everything perfectly.

People move, people pass away and for some products such as children's products or sporting goods, eventually the customers outgrow the need for certain products. Depending on the type of business you are in you might lose 10-20% of your customers every year for one reason or another. Which means that you have to find ways to replace those customers with new ones through marketing and advertising.

Because of this businesses try to do everything in their power to keep their existing customers happy and away from their competition. It is a well-known fact that if you give a customer a reason to look elsewhere, they eventually will. Even if they have been doing business with you for years, if they find a better deal, they will move from you to someone else.

Studies have shown that it makes economic sense to keep existing customers happy as well. It can cost up to 10 times more to bring a new customer through the doors than it costs to keep an existing customer happy. So the economics make a clear case for creating the very best customer experience possible even if it costs money to do so.

The effect of losing customers can also have a ripple effect on the business as well. Fewer customers mean less sales which means less revenue. But it can also mean fewer items ordered and higher prices because you are ordering less quantities. So not only are you selling fewer products you are making less per product. So you are getting hit in the pocketbook twice.

Then there is the competition to consider. Every day good businessmen are looking for a way to become better than their competition. That might mean lower prices and better selection but it also means a better customer experience and creating a customer friendly business. They are working on this every single day so their businesses can grow and become even more competitive.

If your company doesn't do the same things in their business they will find themselves falling behind because others did something while they did nothing. That can present a very real danger. Once customers figure out that another business is offering better products at lower prices with better service guess where they are going to go?

For every customer that goes to the competition, you get penalized twice. You lose that customers business while someone else gains it and all the advantages that go along with it. As other businesses grow they become harder and harder to compete against. Just ask the thousands of hardware stores and lumber yards that went out of business when the large home improvement chains came into town.

So we need to stop for a moment and ask ourselves whether or not we are doing enough to keep our customers happy and coming back again and again. We need to ask ourselves if there was anything else we could have done to keep a customer in our business so they don't go somewhere else. We need to ask ourselves just how committed we are to our customers on a daily basis.

But it is not just the company that has to show commitment to the customer. It also must come from each and every employee because those are the people who are on the front lines and interact with our customers every single day. These are the people who answer questions, make recommendations and solve their problems. These people are the face of the company. Not the owner or the CEO up in his office. But you, the employee who goes face to face with the customer every single day.

It is your attitude and commitment that can make all the difference in the world. It is the things you do that can turn an unhappy customer into a customer for life when they are made to feel appreciated.

It is you who can go the extra mile and do something over the top for a customer so they feel important and valued. It is you who can say "YES!" instead of now and make someone happy in an instant.

These are not difficult things to do. All it takes is a mindset that is dedicated to getting things done and going the extra mile. All it takes are employees that think about how they can get something done instead of why they can't do something. All it takes is a commitment to the customer and their needs. It's a small thing that can pack huge rewards for both you and your business.

Before we go on to the next chapter I would like everyone reading this book to stop for a moment and think about what you just read. Think about how important what you do is to both the customer and the company. Think about how you can help make the company stronger and increase its growth just by changing a few little things you do that can significantly improve the customer experience.

Remember we are all links in the customer service experience and the entire experience can go through without a problem or crash and burn depending on what we do.

Just think about it for a minute or two. Then we will look at exactly what our customers really are. I think a few things just might surprise you!

What is a Customer?

If we are going to really make a commitment to create the best possible customer experience, sometimes it helps to understand exactly what a customer is. Because a customer is more than just someone who walks in through your doors or visits your website and purchases your products and services.

Your customer is the life blood of your business. Without customers your business will fail. Without customers there would be no revenue. Without revenue there would be no profits. Without profits there would be no money to pay salaries and other expenses. So the final result is that without customers your job would cease to exist.

I guess that last statement should put things into proper perspective.

Some people think of customers as special people with special needs that they need to address. While this might be the case with a few customers, the real truth is that our customers are people just like you and I.

Our customers have pretty much the same needs as we do and we want the same things out of doing business with a company.

You yourself are a customer whenever you buy something from someone so it should stand to reason that your customers are normal people just like everyone else. Granted some are going to be nicer than others and some are going to be very difficult. But that is true in all of life not just in business. We all know people who are great to be with and others you try to stay away from as much as possible. Those people are customers as well.

This is a great thing because it gives us insight into what our customers want and what we need or should be doing to make their experience as positive as possible. Because your customers are very similar to you, all you have to do is put yourself in their place to decide what is the best thing to do or the best way to resolve a problem.

For example, if a customer has a problem and you can place yourself in their shoes and determine what it is that you would like to see happen it is a pretty good starting point. If you need to say something to a customer and you can say those words to yourself and determine what your reaction might be, this is a good filter to use when choosing wording,

Another aspect of a customer is that customers are usually people with choices.

Just like you have a choice where to buy your groceries and clothing, so do your customers have choices regarding where they do business. Just like you they do not always concentrate just on price but on the overall experience and value that they receive when they make a purchase.

So let's take a look at a few things that our customers are to our business:

Reason We Are Employed

Like we said, customers make our company and jobs possible. When you look at them in this manner they have an entirely different level of importance to us. Since we sometimes treat people according to the value we place on them, it is important that we understand their importance to our jobs and to our company.

Worthy of Our Respect

Just like you would like to be treated with dignity and respect, our customers want that as well. You might even say they demand it because they have options and can always go elsewhere and take their business with them.

Free to Do Business Wherever they Want

Unless there is nowhere else that people can buy what you sell, meaning that you have a monopoly, people are free to buy whatever they want wherever they want. There is no such thing as forced customer loyalty. Eventually most people will go wherever they feel they get the best overall experience. That is why provide a unique and positive customer experience is so important.

People Just Like You and I

This is important so we will repeat this once more. Customers are just people like you and I with the same wants, needs and desires. So it should not be a mystery as to what your customers want. Needs and wants will vary from customer to customer as they do from person to person but the core things will remain the same.

People Who Want to Be Appreciated

At the very core of most people is a need or desire to feel appreciated by others and this includes customers as well. They want to feel that their business is appreciated and valued by the business as well as their employees. This is why so many business require their employees thank every customer as they complete their purchases or as they leave the store.

It is amazing how much this means to some people. It is a small gesture but one that can bring huge benefits in the minds of the customer. Just saying "thank you" and "have a nice day" takes only a few seconds but can help make someone feel good and appreciated.

What are customers are is very important but the flip side is also important as well. What our customers should not be thought or can make all the difference in the world. As you read some of these items I am sure you will be able to recall when you witnessed some of these behaviors in your experiences as well and how they made you feel. If you remember that these items should really come to life for you!

An Inconvenience

Our customers represent the overall success and profit of our business. They are the reason our business and jobs exist. So it just makes sense that you do not treat them as an inconvenience. You should not look up at them and frown or shake your head or make them feel like it is an imposition to you to help them.

That means putting down the donut or sandwich and helping the customer. You can finish you snack later.

The same thing with the cigarette or coffee. Those things should not be your focus. Your focus should be on the customer first and everything else should come after.

You should not make your personal phone calls or conversations take precedence over your customers and you should not make them feel that they are interrupting something that you feel is more important than they are. Every customer should be made to feel like they are the most important person or thing in your positon. Because they are the reason you are there in the first place, they should be your top priority.

People Who Are Tolerated

A lot can be said without a single word being spoken. You should never feel that customers are people that have to be tolerated because that is going to reveal itself in your expressions and your attitude. We have all seen the cashier or salesperson that just doesn't want to be bothered but has to help you because that's their job.

Instead of making people feel like they are being tolerated we should make them feel that we are eager to help them. We should approach them not wait for them to approach us. We should ask them if they need help and not the other way around. In other words, we should be pro-active with all our customers and make every effort to make sure they get the best level of service possible.

A Distraction

Sometimes people have to multi-task in their jobs because they have more to do than just help customers. Maybe they have to run reports or fill out paperwork or stock shelves or take inventory. While all of those tasks and responsibilities are important, we must always remember that the customer should always be our top priority.

We should never make people wait while we finish a form or unload that full box of product and place it on the shelves. While it might be OK to finish counting that last row of product during inventory, even then we can be pro-active and let the customers know that we will be with them in a minute.

An Annoyance

Last, but most certainly not least, your customers should never be made to feel that they are an annoyance to you. If you dislike dealing with customers, that is your right to feel that way but it also means that you are in the wrong job or career. You should enjoy interacting with people and helping them with whatever their needs might be at that point in time.

You should make people feel that you are interested in them and that their needs are important to you.

Spend the time you need to really help the customer and not try to rush them out the door or make them feel that you would much rather be doing something else.

When customers have problems, you need to understand that those problems are important to them. You should want to help resolve those problems and not make the customer feel that they are not important. You should make the customer feel that you have an honest desire to help them resolve their problems and make them go away.

As you should easily see by this point, it is easy to know what a customer wants and needs because those are probably the same things you would want as well. You should also see how your behavior and attitude is going to effect your ability to help the customer and either add or subtract from the customer experience.

But most important at this point is that you understand what a customer is and what a customer should not be. Because that is the basis of everything that is going to follow as far as the customer experience is concerned. If you are still not clear as far as what our customers represent to us and our businesses, I strongly suggest you go back and re-read this chapter until it all becomes clear to you. Once you are able to understand all of this in its proper perspective then everything else will fall into place.

What Customers Really Want

If you ask people what their customers want when they call or walk in and you will get various replies. They will tell you that customers want to know which product to buy or where something is located or to help them with a defective product or just answer a simple question. And all of those answers would be correct.

But all of those answers also have something in common. All of those answers contain one factor that is the basis for every customer need that walks through the door. All of those answers point towards one basic need.

All of those answers point to a problem that the customer needs to have addressed or resolved.

Customers buy products or come into our businesses because they have a problem that they cannot resolve by themselves.

They either need a product or advice or some kind of assistance from us. When they get that advice or assistance and their problem is resolved, they are happy. When their problems are not resolved completely, they are not satisfied. This is the most basic way to look at all customer needs.

Sometimes the customers don't know what their real problems are. They think they know but they only see the need not the problem. When that happens sometimes their decisions might address the need but not the problem. While that might sound confusing, let's look at an example.

A customer comes in to buy a washing machine. They are looking for a washing machine because their current model is not doing a good job cleaning their clothes, especially their son's football uniform. So they are looking for a new clothes washer.

But their problem is not that they need a new washing machine. That is their need. Their problem is that their current model is not getting their clothes clean. That's a significant difference because it might indicate that they need a better or more advanced machine with added capacity or cleaning ability to handle that football uniform.

If you look at the need you might sell them the unit that is on sales because it represents the best price or best value. But if you look at the problem, you might see that the lower priced model will not have the cleaning capacity to resolve their problem.

So they might buy the machine, get it home, use it and still have the not fully clean uniform and still have the same problem.

In order to make our customers happy both while they are in the middle of the sales process and afterwards, we have to solve their problems AND address their needs. Sometimes this is not always easy when they want something that is not going to solve their problems.

For example, in the example we just used, suppose the customer insisted on buying the cheapest model even though it did not have what it takes to solve their problem. You know that when they get home and find their new washer doesn't get the uniform clean they are going to come back and complain and probably blame it all on you or the salesperson that sold it to them.

So first and foremost, our customers want to get their problems solved. But they also want other things as well that are all related to the customer service experience. Here are a few of the most important things our customers look for in a sales person or a company they want to do business with. To have any chance of getting that customer to be one of your customers, you are going to have to provide most or all of the following to the customer.

Honesty

Customers want someone they can trust. They want someone who will show them and recommend the best product for their needs not the product that pays them the largest commission or has the highest mark-up.

They also want someone who is going to do the right thing by them even if it does take a little bit longer or requires more effort. They want to believe that the person who is helping them has an actual desires to really help them.

Respect

This is a basic way to treat everyone not just customers. Everyone should be treated with dignity and respect even though they might not treat us that way. When it comes to customer treating people with respect makes any situation better and less difficult to resolve.

That means not talking down to customers or belittling them or yelling at them. It means listening to them when they have something to say and not cutting them off in mid-sentence because you are done listening to them.

Friendliness

Everyone likes to deal with happy and smiling people and customers are no different when it comes to this. While customers are not looking for someone to become their best friend or fishing buddy they are looking for someone who is pleasant to deal with.

That means putting a smile on your face and speaking in a happy tone whenever you are talking with a customer. It means letting them know you like your job and like dealing with customers. If you cannot project this to customers you just might not be cut out for customer service work.

Concern

A customer who has a problem wants to interact with someone who honestly wants to help them. They want that person to show some concern regarding the problems and what has to be done to correct it.

You can show concern by asking a lot of questions and taking the time to listen to the answers. You can also show concern by working with the customer to make sure they get the best resolution as possible even if it means going the extra mile to do so.

Timeliness

This is another basic part of showing respect to others. Be on time. If you say you are going to meet a customer at 1 o'clock, then be there at 12:50 not 1:10. If you tell them you will call them by 5PM, do not call then at 1PM the next day. If you are supposed to start your shift at noon, don't waltz in at 12:15 like everything is perfectly fine.

Granted at times things will come up that will delay you. But if you take a minute to notify the customer, or at least apologize to them for the delay, most people will understand this. Unless, of course, you make a habit out of being late and inconsiderate.

Courteous

Customers also like people to be courteous when interacting with them. Unless the customer tells you they should not be referred to by their first name unless you have already established that relationship. In other words, you should call a customer "Mr. James" and not "Ted" unless you are 100% sure that is what the customer wants.

Compassion

Customers also want people with compassion when it comes to solving problems. That doesn't mean you have to take responsibility for the problem. But it does mean letting the customer know that you are sorry that they are having this problem and that you want to do whatever you can to help them resolve it.

This just means that they want you to show them that you care, that you really want to help them and that you are willing to do your best on their behalf. That really is not a lot to ask when it comes to how you treat a customer.

Accuracy

Even the best or well-intentioned information will not make someone happy if it is incorrect. A customer want accurate and factual information. They are looking for guesswork or personal opinions. They are looking for factual information based on your education and experience. In other words, what you think something should be is not enough. You need to KNOW something and not THINK that something is right.

That means not guessing and instead asking someone else or do some basic research. It means developing thorough product knowledge so that when someone asks you a question you know the answer. It means become an expert or an authority in your field. It means becoming known as the "go-to" person for certain questions or assistance.

Technical or Product Knowledge

Though it should be common sense to expect a salesperson or an employee to have actual product knowledge, this is not always the case. Once I asked a question of a salesperson only to have him take out a copy of the manual and try to look it up. While I appreciated the fact that he wanted to find out the right answer and not guess, I was less than thrilled that he did not know the answer.

At least he could have read the manual in the stockroom in the back and pretended to know the answer.

All of these attributes and qualities are what our customers are looking for. Most of them are common sense and the appropriate way to treat or interact with any human being while some might be job or career specific. Whatever the case might be, the more of these qualities that you can provide the better customer experience you will be able to provide to every customer.

But some of those qualities are contained in the attitude that you have towards your customers and that is what we are going to start working on right now.

The True Value of a Customer

The thing about our brains is that they usually treat other people and things according to the worth that it assigns to them. The greater the worth or value the more attention we will pay to that person or object. So it stands to reason that if we see something as more valuable we will pay more attention to it and treat it better.

For those of you who might disagree, let me ask you this question:

If it is raining hard outside and you had to run to get to your car and on the way you saw a nice shiny nickel lying on the ground would you stop and pick it up? You might on a nice and sunny day but when it's raining hard it just isn't worth stopping and getting soaked.

But if you in the same hard rain and you're running to the same car and you saw a $100 bill lying on the ground in the exact same spot where that nickel was, you probably would stop and pick it up. Why? Because it had more value and the higher value made it worthwhile for you to get a little bit wetter in order to get a $100.

If you are being honest with yourself right now you are agreeing that you would probably do the exact same thing. You would pass up the nickel but stop to grab the $100 bill. That is because your brain told you that there was enough value in stopping to make it worthwhile. The same thing applies to our customers and how we treat them.

One common problem many people have in understanding the real value of a customer. Some people go by the value of the current sale while others might set an arbitrary value based on their experience in what an average customer might buy during their usual visit. But it might surprise you that by following that evaluation process that you are doing both you and your customers a huge disservice.

There are several factors that make up the real value of every customer. Once you understand all of these factors you will have a much more accurate feeling about exactly how much your customers are worth to you and your company.

Some of the most important things to consider when establishing the value of a customer are:

Current Amount of Sale

Though this is a very short-sighted view of customer value or worth, the amount of the current sale does factor into the equation only as it can relate to future potential sales. But even when you remove that from the equation let's be honest. You can going to value a $5,000 sale much more than you are a $50 sales because those types of high value sales happen much less frequently.

Prior Sales

They say a lot in life can be predicted based on what a person has done in the past. We can use that philosophy when it comes to purchases as well. If a customer has come into your store 4 times a month for the last several years and spent $100 each time then you can reasonably predict that they will continue to do so in the near future.

Of course, this might not be true if the products you sell have an age limitation or other factor that might influence how long a customer might use your product. For example, if someone has purchased a gallon of milk a week for the last 5 years, chances are they will do so for the next year or more as well because people need milk for all or most of their lives.

But just because someone purchased $100 worth of diapers a month for the last 3 years does not mean they will continue to do so because eventually they will have no further need for that product.

But for most products that have a long life span you should factor in the amount of business the customer has done with you for at least one year but 3-5 years would be a better and more accurate reflection of future business.

Future Sales

Unless the products you sell are none shot purchases that are rarely repeated, you will need to factor in the potential business this customer is likely to bring to your company in the next year or two as well. This is important because to just count the most recent sale would make you severely underestimated the true value this customer represents to your business.

Up to this point we are talking about things that can be measured or predicted based on past and current purchases. You can take this information and accurately determine what this customer is likely to spend in your business in the next year or two. After all, you are using known behavior and actual figures in your calculations But now let's talk about one final factor you need to consider that might be even more important than any of the other factors.

That factor is:

Referral or Recommended Sales

Every time you make a customer happy or unhappy they will tell people about their experience. Happy people talk up your business and recommend it to others. Unhappy people talk down about your business and try to keep people away from it. We know this happens so that is not up for discussion. But the one factor we don't know is how many people your current customer will talk to about your business and how much those comments will impact your sales.

We do know that angry people are up to 10 times more likely to spread the word than happy people. Angry people want to tell the world while happy people sometimes take things for granted and might not tell anyone unless they are specifically asked. That's the problem because you never can know if that customer you just made very happy is going to tell 5 people or 500 about your business.

To make matters more confusing and vague, you will never know if those 5 or 500 people each spent $5 or $5,000 with your company! That is one reason why selling customer service to some companies is so difficult!

We know the benefits are there and we know that certain behaviors happens after the sale but there is no way to place an accurate or concrete number on it.

So now that you know what goes into evaluating the true value of a customer, let's look at an example to drive this message home.

Alice walks into a sandwich shop and orders a sandwich which she takes back to her office. She paid $5 for the sandwich but the sandwich was horrible. The meat was too fatty and appeared to be quite old as well. The bread was stale and there was very little meat on the sandwich.

So Alice goes back to ask for a new sandwich. The clerk, seeing the $5 cost of the sale treats Alice based on that value and refuses to make her a new sandwich stating there was nothing wrong with it and asking her what she expected for just $5. Alive is angry and walks out. The clerk laughs it off and thinks it's no big deal because it was a $5 sale so who care if she comes back.

But here is where it gets interesting because this is a true story although "Alice" was not her real name. But what followed did happen.

Alice goes back and tells her co-workers about how she was treated. Since they all go to that shop a few times a week, and since this shop did their office catering, they were a bit surprised.

But the next time Alice wanted a sandwich she went to another shop a bit further away. She got a really, really good sandwich for the same price. But the sandwich had twice the meat, the meat was a higher quality and Alice was very happy.

People see the sandwich and asked where Alive got it. She told them of this other store and one by one, the other people tried that store, liked the sandwiches better, and started going there for lunch. And when the next catering event was ordered, it went to the new shop with the better quality product.

Now in this case, a $5 sandwich caused a single customer to go elsewhere. But the larger impact came from the other people who also stopped going there and went somewhere else as well. So that $5 a week turned in $55 dollars a week and the lost catering cost them roughly $2,500 for the year.

The valuation of the customer based on the single sale was $5. Not very high and not all that much concern over her leaving.

The future business of $5 a week for 50 weeks places her valuation at $250 a year which might have made the person behind the counter give her another sandwich.

But the referral business it cost them was over $2,750 a year which definitely would have made the person provide a free sandwich to Alive because her value was known to be worth it to do so.

So when you add it all together, you could say that the refusal to make her a new $5 sandwich cost that business over $5,000! All because someone was so short sighted that they didn't stop to factor in the true value that Alice represented to their business. And this lost business was only for the first year! How much more business would that sandwich shop lose because other people Alive told then went ahead and told others! And then who knows how many people those people told and so on and so on!

The problem is that when you underestimate the value of a customer you cannot make accurate and proper informed decisions when it comes to how to treat that customer. Options that would be out of the question for a customer worth $5 might be slam dunks for a customer worth $5,000. But only when the people involved really understood that this customer was really worth $5,000 to the business.

In customer service we are asked or expected to make these kinds of decisions each and every day. Part of the decision making process requires that we understand the situation and the customers involved.

Then we should be asking ourselves if this makes sense after all the information is considered. If we have all the information, and we know the real worth of that customer, then we can make the right decision. If we don't have all the information, or if we have the wrong information, we will often make the wrong decision.

Would you lose a $50,000 customer over a $5 dispute?

Probably not.

Customers vs. the Company

We are going to switch gears a bit now and talk about responsibility to both the customer and the company. While most customers do not care about the company and its policies, the fact is you MUST think about them as you interact with the customer. Because if you don't you can place the future of the company in danger.

One hard fact in business is that if you want to help your customers and continue to serve them in the future, your company must remain in existence in order to do so. That means you should always be considering the impact of your actions and decisions on the company as well as the customer. It is sort of a balancing act making sure that the resolution makes sense for both sides.

In the last chapter we discussed the value of a customer and how that relates to how we treat them. It also relates to what we offer them in terms of resolutions when they have a problem. Though some of you might not think that is fair and that everyone should be treated equally, well, while that's certainly admirable it is not reality.

But that also doesn't mean that we give away the entire store for even our best customers. Even with our largest customers there should be limits and those limits should make sense. We should do whatever it takes to keep every customer happy as long as we meet two criteria.

First, we need to make sure we are acting within the law and giving the customer what they are entitled to under the law. We must do that whether or not it makes sense to do so or we will find ourselves in trouble with the law. What the customer is entitled to under the law is the minimum of what we need to do to keep them happy. Anything less is a violation of the law and anything more we do is strictly an added benefit we choose to provide.

Second, we should always look at each customer and each situation carefully before making a decision. Every customer is different and every situation is different as well so there is no way you can have one resolution or action that will work 100% of the time.

Customer service is not a black and white process. In fact, it is mostly gray area where people must think, evaluate and make decisions based on the information available at the time.

Our final decision should make sense from the company point of view as well. While we want the customer to be happy we also want and need to protect the business as well. We cannot afford to give every customer a resolution that costs the company 20 times what that customer is worth. That is just not financially prudent.

When we are presented with a situation that requires some sort of resolution, we need to thoroughly evaluate it and ask ourselves the following questions:

Is the Situation Legitimate?

The first thing we need to make sure of is that the situation really is as the customer claims it is. Some people are known to lie through their teeth to get something they want and don't want to pay for. So if the customer is at fault that needs to be factored in.

But even if the customer is at fault you need to determine whether or not you want to anger that customer and lose his future business. So in some cases we would actually give the customer an offer for something that they caused. It's not a question of right or wrong. Instead it is all about keeping the customer satisfied when it makes sense to do so.

Are the Demands Reasonable?

Just because a customer demands something or feels entitled to it does not make it reasonable. Many customers have been known to demand the moon and the sky for something trivial or even non-existent. When you ask a customer why they want what they said and their only reply is because they feel they are entitled to it that can cause a problem.

The demand should be reasonable for the situation involved. If you make a mistake that costs someone a lot of time and inconvenience or a mistake that caused damage or injury, that is one thing and you should fact all of that into your decision. Or, if your error resulted in the customer incurring additional costs because of that mistake, that should be factored in as well.

But if a customer purchases something that turns out to be defective requiring them to come in to get a replacement, you should not pay them for pain and suffering and emotional distress and sessions with a therapist. Part of life is going through little inconveniences like that and this is not something that usually requires a large offer of restitution.

There should be reasons for any demands that exceed what most people would feel is a fair and reasonable settlement.

If those reasons are not apparent and the customer cannot give you those reasons or explain the reasons they are asking for what they are asking for, then those demands usually can be set to the side as you work on what is real and appropriate.

What Does the Law Say?

Note: We are not lawyers and do not pretend to be. Therefore any specific information pertaining to the law and your actions under it should be directed to a lawyer in your state. The following is just our opinion as it relates to customer service and not to the legal specifics of the situation.

Regardless of what we want or think is fair or what makes sense to the company, the law is the law and we must abide by it and follow it to the letter. If the law says a customer has certain rights then you must make sure you adhere to those rights and treat the customer accordingly. You cannot rewrite the law for each customer according to their own value to the business. The law is a minimum standard of treatment. You can go above and beyond if you want to but you cannot provide less.

Another interesting factor of the law is how it can impact your decisions on other situations as well. The law says everyone needs to be treated fairly and in the same manner. So if you make a large settlement to a few customers and then decline that same settlement to another customer, they can use that against you in a court of law.

So, if you want to make a different settlement to one customer, make sure you have a valid reason for it that can be explained should this matter go to court. There will always be a percentage of customers who will look for any reason at all to take the company to court in the hopes that a large settlement is in their future. Unfortunately, there are also a lot of lawyers who have the same hopes and are all too willing to present those cases in a courtroom.

Does it Make Sense for the Business?

At this point we want to understand if what we want to do makes sense to the business. Is the cost of the settlement in line with the value of the customer? Does it meet the minimum legal standards that we have to abide by? Is the business capable of withstanding the financial impact of the settlement?

Plus, we also have to be concerned with setting a precedent for future settlements as well. Customers are people and people talk to each other. If you do one thing for Jim and Jim talks about it to others, they are going to want the same things you gave Jim. Ask yourself how the business could handle those requests. They may never come but you need to make your decisions thinking that they eventually will.

What Are Our Options?

There are very few situations where there are not several options available to us. So the idea here is to try and find the best overall situation that costs the company the least amount of money while still being an appropriate response.

For example, if the customer is asking for a monetary settlement but we can offer free services instead, that might be more appealing to the customer while costing the business less in the long run. For example, if the customer is demanding $250 in cash but you can offer them $500 in free carpet cleaning or other service, the cost of providing that "free" service is much less than the $250 refund.

Always look at all the options and try to find the one that costs the company the least while still making the customer happy. That is the resolution you should lead with and present to the customer. Then you go from there depending on how the customer reacts.

Is it a Win-Win for Everyone?

The other thing we should always look for is that whatever we do or however we react that we try to give the customer as much of what they want or need while protecting the business at the same time. Customer service should not be a win-lose situation where the company tries to do the least possible or try and cheat their customers. Instead they should always be looking for ways to give the customer as much of what they want as possible.

That is how you create loyal and long-term customers.

Policies and Procedures

Because every situation and every customer is different, we need to have a way of making sure that everyone is treated fairly and properly as well as within the law. Since there is no way we can expect every employee to have the knowledge to accomplish this, a company will develop and institute policies and procedures to help them interact with customers.

The larger the company the more policies and procedures they might have and those policies and procedures might be more detailed and specific. This is done because the larger a company is the more impact their decisions can be.

Sometimes it might appear that there are too many rules, policies and procedures and that they interfere with you doing you jobs.

Some of these rules might even appear to have no reason behind them as well. But keep in mind that every rule, policy or procedure is in place because at one time or another something happened that the company did not want to happen again. Maybe it caused them legal problems, maybe the decision cost them a lot of money or it was for some other reason.

But contrary to popular belief, these rules, policies and procedures are not there just to make your life and job harder. They are there for legitimate reasons. You might not understand what those reasons might be, but they are there.

Trust me on that.

A perfect example of a policy is a return policy. Setting a limit on the time a person can return a product for a refund makes sense for both the company and the customer as long as the time frame is relatively fair. That is because the longer period of time the customer can return a product the larger the financial exposure the company has for those returned products. This results in higher costs of doing business which results in higher prices to the customers. So limiting the time lowers the exposure and lowers prices as well.

The policies and procedures should be in a company or employee manual so that every employee can be aware of them. Usually you do not have to know or memorize all of them because not every one will pertain to your particular job. But you will have to learn the ones that do pertain to your job so you know to follow them when the situation dictates.

If such a manual is not available you should ask your manager or supervisor about any policy or procedure that pertains to your job. If they are not available in writing then take notes as he or she explains them to you. Make sure you know them and understand them and how to use them. If something is unclear, then ask for clarification so you know what to do and when to do it.

As far as customers are concerned, be prepared for one thing when it comes to rules, policies and procedures.

That is that your customer is not going to care at all what your company tells you that you have to do. They are going to want what they want regardless of what your rules tell you to do. Because of this you cannot hide behind a rule or policy. You are going to have to give other reasons for your actions or decisions and hope that those reasons hold up in the mind of the customer.

So do not use policies and procedures as an excuse for anything.

You can use them as a reason such as when a customer tries to return something they bought 120 days ago and your company has a 90 day return limit. In that case it was a clearly stated policy that probably is posted somewhere in a prominent location in the store.

The same might go for a policy where only store credit is given on returns and not a cash refund. Though your customers probably weren't aware of this policy because they thought it would never come to using it, you can show them the clearly stated policy as a reason for not issuing them a cash refund.

Well-crafted policies and procedures are almost always within the law and usually go above what the law dictates. What that means is that these are company mandated parameters within which you are to act. But it also means that the company is free to make changes to those rules on an individual basis with approval from a manager or supervisor.

The best way to handle disputes stemming from policies and procedures is to act within them and see if you can resolve the situation within those guidelines. If that is not possible then you would go to your boss, manager or supervisor to see if your suggested plan of action could be approved.

Maybe you decide the customer should get a cash refund or maybe that 120 day return should be processed. But those are not your decisions to make. So consult whoever you need to consult to get their approval.

One last thing about policies and procedures.

Many times policies and procedures become outdates over time. The original reasons for them might have changed or no longer exist. When this happens either policies lose their effectiveness and might even have a negative impact on how the business is run. When this occurs, the smart thing to do is make your manager or supervisor aware of the issue and let them handle it.

But always keep in mind that it is your duty and responsibility to stay within the parameters of every rule, policy and procedure. They are there for a reason and it is not up to you or any other employee to operate outside of them unless that action is approved by a manager or supervisor.

The Importance of

Listening

As a customer service representative, or with anyone who interacts with customers at all for any reason, you must understand the importance of listening. Listening is one part of the communication process that most people do not concentrate on or understand the importance of. Without knowing how to listen effectively you will always be operating at a disadvantage when it comes to the communication process.

Most people do not understand that over half of what we communicate to other people is not contained in the words we speak. In some cases the spoken words account for only a minor part of the message we deliver. The rest is contained in the way we speak, the expressions we use and the tone of our voice.

It is through those factors that the bulk of what we are saying is actually conveyed.

Think about that for a minute. Think about how we can use facial expressions and other physical indicators to help us interact better with our customers. Unless we are interacting with customers over the phone we almost always see them before speaking with them. That means we can see their expressions, watch the way they walk and move and get a preview, or advanced notice, as to how they are feeling. This will enable us to change our approach based on their emotions.

Every situation or interaction starts off at a particular emotional point. If everyone is happy the conversation will be light and positive. But if some of the people are angry, the conversation might take on a confrontational tone. By this I am sure you would agree that we would handle both conversations a bit differently because of emotions.

You might be a bit carefree and even joke around a bit when you are happy. But those same comments and attitude might work against you when someone is angry. So we need to be able to "listen" with our eyes as well as our ears.

So that we might get a better insight into how we need to listen to the entire message, here are a few of the main things we need to concentrate on when "listening" to a customer or anyone else for that matter:

Words

Of course the words we use help us verbally deliver the actual message in a way that is almost universally understood. For example, the words, "This doesn't work and I would like a refund" clearly tells the problem and the desired outcome. Frowning and handing the product to someone indicates you are not happy but little else.

So we need to listen to the words that are being spoken so we understand that part of the message. But we should not stop there because there is a lot more of the message that is there to understand.

Tone

The tone of voice helps us determine whether the person is really upset, just annoyed or is taking the whole matter in stride and considers it part of life. This will help us decide the best way to approach the situation from our side.

Tone also helps us gauge the seriousness of the situation as well. If someone is truly upset there could be other things going on as well that we need to prepare for and take into consideration. For example maybe the lamp they bought broke and that might not be a big deal. But when it broke if it fell over on one of their small children, that's another matter entirely.

Emotion

You can also see emotion in the color of the skin and how a person moves and looks. Noticing this can alert us to the need of becoming a lot more careful in both our approach and determining which words to use.

For example, if a customer walks through the doors with tears in their eyes, you can instantly tell that this customer is extremely upset or that something serious has happened that you need to be aware of. You would then be very careful on what you said and how you treated this customer. You would also take steps to calm the customer down as well.

Facial Expressions

Facial expressions are a wonderful way of not only seeing how someone feels at that moment but also how they react to certain things you do and say. Their words might be saying one thing but their expressions might be saying something else.

Watching facial expressions as we talk to customers is also interesting as well because their reactions might give us some insight into the real truth behind the problem. For example, if you think they caused the problem and mention that and they get all nervous and fidgety, that might tell you that you are completely right and they are lying.

Any time someone gets nervous or evasive they will often give their fears away in their eyes. If you cannot make eye contact with a customer while they are talking to you changes are they have something to hide or that they are being somewhat less than truthful.

Body Language

The way we carry ourselves tells a lot about our moods and character as well. People who walk straight upright tend to be more confident and secure than someone who slouches over. Someone who is leaning in might indicate aggression or confidence as well. A firm handshake indicates power and confidence.

Holding your head up high indicates confidence while hanging your head down often indicates shyness or weakness. Looking people straight in the eye while talking indicates someone who is to be reckoned with or taken seriously. People who refuse to look you in the eye might be either very shy, intimidated or less than honest.

The point is looking at people when we are interacting with them will give us a look into how they really feel rather than just taking what they say for face value.

Just like a poker player watches the faces of people they are playing against, so do we look at the faces of people we are talking to in hopes of learning a little more about the situation.

Gestures

Gestures are a great way of seeing how someone is feeling. If they are gesturing wildly they are either very angry, very passionate or extremely excited and happy. Looking at the face will often let you know why the gestures are there. But gestures can also give you more information than the words might be able to.

For example, if you say something was "medium size" than that would signify that it was larger than some things and smaller than others but that still leaves a wide possible range of sizes. But if those words were accompanied by a gesture of two hands that were a certain distance apart, that would be a more accurate indication of size.

Gestures can indicate size, express emotional level and provide other descriptive purposes. Gestures can also help with direction such as pointing to something we want someone to look at or serve other purposes. Gestures are just one more way people can express themselves and deliver their messages. Depending on the person gestures might be very common for them or very rare and are only used when emotions are running high. That is why it sometimes helps to know the person so you can more accurately interpret the gestures.

Now all people are not going to necessarily use all of the forms of delivering their messages. Some people are extremely good at keep facial expressions neutral so they do not give away their true reactions. Other people may use gestures all the time like your "always talking with his hands Uncle Frank" who cannot say two words without using his hands.

For some people certain gestures or actions might mean something totally different than they do for other people. Because of this it is not a good idea to make a final judgment or jump to conclusions based on just one thing. Instead, the best way to listen to someone is to hear the words and them use expressions, tone, emotions and everything else and draw a conclusion based on everything instead of just one thing.

It is important to always be aware of all of these factors as they can also signal a change in emotion or attitude as the conversation moves forward. You might see signs of relaxing or people getting less angry which would tell you to keep doing what you are doing because it is working.

Or you might see signs of people becoming angrier or tense which would tell you that you need to stop what you are doing and find another approach that will have the desired effect. It is all in the interpretation and judgment of the people involved. In other words it is not an exact science and you are going to have to learn how to use and interpret this information correctly. But the really obvious signs are there is you just know what to look for. So use those first and move on to the others as your skills and abilities allow.

Distractions

Now that we understand how to listen effectively, let's take things one step further and talk about the major roadblock to effective communications. That roadblock are the distractions that can be present that prevent everyone from communicating effectively.

Distractions are all over and most of them we don't even realize. Though it is not possible to list every distraction, here are a few of the major ones and how they can impact the communication process:

Computers

If you are talking to someone, look at them and not your computer monitor. You cannot surf the web and carry on a conversation and contrite on both at the same time.

Trying to do so prohibits you from looking at who you are talking to so you will miss the physical signs of communication.

Not only that but it is just rude to not pay attention when someone is speaking to you. You might just as well tell them that whatever they are saying to you is not so valuable to you it deserves your undivided attention. Consider how that message will be received by others.

Cell Phone or Regular Phones

You also cannot carry on two conversations at the same time so unless your phone conversation is part of your in-person conversation or vice versa, either call the person you are on the phone with back or tell the person standing in front of you that you will talk to him in a few minutes.

Trying to talk to two people at once sends the same message as all other forms of multi-tasking sends. That they or their message are not worth your undivided attention.

E-Mail or Texting

Don't e-mail or text people while you are talking.

Not only is it extremely rude but it prevents you from see and hearing all parts of the information the other person is giving you. The result might be making the wrong decision based on incomplete information and making a problem worse that it should be. Even if that doesn't happen, it is just extremely ultra-rude.

Background Noise

Noise is one of the largest distractions there is because it prevents people from hearing all the words that are being spoken. Whenever you don't hear something your brain tries to fill in the blanks made by the missing words. The more blanks the more guesswork and the more guesswork the more opportunity for errors and confusion.

If you are in a noisy or distracting area, try to move the conversation to a quieter area. If you are in your office and outside noises are coming through, then get up and close the door. In other words, do everyone a favor and try to create the most noise free environment possible for your communication.

If that is not possible and the conversation must take place where you are, then stop frequently and ask if everyone heard you OK or if there was any confusion. Do not rely on people stopping you when they cannot hear because they will be hesitant to do so at times. Be pro-active and ask people whether they can hear you OK.

Multi-Tasking

Many of these distractions occur because too many people think they can do too many things at the same time without the quality of anything suffering. While they might think that facts dictate otherwise.

Whenever our brain has to separate its resources to do more than one task at a time its abilities become compromised. If we are talking and e-mailing, both are compromised. If we are talking and texting or watching television, both are compromised. We might think we are hearing everything but the brain skips over some things because it is busy doing something else. You might not realize it but it happens.

How others the respect they deserve by giving them your total and undivided attention. Concentrate on what they are saying and how they look while they are saying it. If you don't understand something, ask a question. Keep asking questions until you are clear what the message is and what it is that you are supposed to do.

The more you leave to chance the greater the possibility for guesswork and interpretation. The more interpretation the greater the likelihood for mistakes. Since mistakes cost us time, money and resources it makes sense to avoid them whenever possible.

Interacting with Different Customers

We mentioned how each customer is different from the next one. But even though personalities can differ we might also have differences among different types of customers. By types I mean age groups, different nationalities and different races as well. All of these groups have different customs, wants, needs and desires. As an employee with direct customer contact, you must be aware of these differences and incorporate them into your approach.

Now let us say right from the start that you must never, ever discriminate against any group of people for any reason. Not only is this against the law but it can cause massive problems for your company in your neighborhood and a reputation that might prove impossible to shake or rehabilitate. You must treat everyone fairly and at the same level at all times.

But that being said, different cultures have different customs and this might require a different approach in order to keep those customers happy. We should also say at this point that even though you need to adapt to these rules and differences does not mean you have to agree with them or believe in them. But you do need to tolerate them.

The first thing every employee should do is find out about the company's customer base. What are their demographics? What different groups are there and what are their differences? Doing a bit of research in the beginning will allow you to stop making innocent mistakes based on ignorance and nothing else. Make it a priority to get to know as much as possible about your customer base.

This might mean trying to learn the basics of another language if a large part of your customer base or local area has people who speak that language. This will just make you more valuable to your customers and your company at the same time. It is also another way to show people that you have an honest desire to help them. Someone who didn't care about a group of people would not make the effort to learn their language. You don't have to become fluent in their language. You just need to know enough to carry on a basic conversation.

This can also help when interacting with the customers and understanding their special needs. That means scheduling deliveries around their religious holidays or obligations. It means knowing when to call them and when not to. This is part making them happy and part respecting their lifestyle as well. Both efforts will be appreciated.

But keep in mind that in problem situations or tense encounters it might be advantageous to escalate the issue to another employee who is better versed in the customer's native language. This can be especially true when people are angry because that is when speech becomes faster and more difficult to understand. To avoid confusion or misunderstanding, get someone who is fluent in their language to either assist or take over for you.

Just remember in the back of your mind that it is up to you to adapt to their culture when it comes to selling them something and not the other way around. This is just one additional way you can show your customers that you appreciate their business. If you are not going to do that chances are someone else will. And they will get your customers because you allowed the door to open.

If you are new to the job or to the company, ask a co-worker about what you might need to know about the customers. But keep an open mind because your co-workers might have a prejudice against someone and will fill you full of inaccurate information.

Listen to what they have to say, take it to heart and sort out the real information from the attitudes and then decide what is really true from your personal experiences.

Cultural and ethnic diversity is becoming a larger and larger issue every year and successful companies are learning how to deal with it and some even use it to their advantage. It is up to you how you wish to approach this issue but always remember you should always be doing your very best towards every customer whether they look or act like you or not.

Looking for the
Win-Win Outcome

A few chapters back, we talked about the win-win resolution and how important it is to customer satisfaction and the overall health of the company. Because it is so important, we figured we should go into a bit more detail so that everyone can embrace this all important concept. That is why we are ending this book with this topic. Because if you just come away from reading this book believing in the importance of the win-win outcome, you will have learned something extremely important.

One of the focus points of any successful business is keeping their customers happy and satisfied. They want to do this because they never want to give any customer even the slightest reason to look elsewhere. It is bad enough that the competition is advertising looking to find ways to get customers to come over to their side.

So businesses never want to make it even a remote possibility that one of their loyal customer would even think about going somewhere else.

The problem is when customers do try somewhere else a certain percentage of them will stick with the new business. They might be treated especially well because they are recognized as a new customer. They might be given discounts or other incentives to come back in the future. Whatever the reason might be or whatever might happen, the key is to stop it before the competition even has a chance.

Because of that we want to be able to give our customers as much of what they want or need as possible. We should not be looking to get away with the cheapest option or the best settlement. Because what might be cheaper now could cost us a fortune later on. So the key is to give people as much as we can while still protecting the interests of the business.

One way we can do that is by listening to the customers to find out what they are really looking for. Sometimes it isn't money. Sometimes it's an added bonus or something added for free. Sometimes the value to the customer can be significantly greater than the cost to the business. But it is the value in the mind of the customer that really counts!

Look for ways to provide more value. Think or services or add-on items that might have a low cost but a high perceived value to the customer. Think about things that might cost the business little or nothing but might make the customer happy. Things like free delivery or a free yearly maintenance or something like that. These are the things that creative businesses do to keep their customers happy.

Some businesses look to meet the expectations of the customer and while that is fine for some customers the much better approach is to try to exceed or beat those expectations. That means giving the customer more than they expected. That means impressing the heck out of them by having them leave with more than they thought they were going to get.

There are a few reasons to do this.

First, anytime you can give someone more than they thought they were going to get they will be happy. That means they are more likely to continue to do business with the company. That means more sales and added profits in the upcoming months or year.

Second, satisfied customer who get what they thought they would get or get what they asked for are often happy but not impressed. Impressed people tend to talk about their experiences while happy people might not. So if you want to get the most benefit out of the situation, really strive to impress the customer to take advantage of word of mouth free advertising.

Third, surprisingly enough, even when you give people what they want they still might be a bit negative because the problem occurred in the first place. If they didn't come out on top in their mind they still might look elsewhere in the future and try somewhere else to avoid future problems. The mind does not always think rationally so the expectation of a problem-free future might be unrealistic, customers still will search for it.

The bottom line is that every employee at every opportunity should be looking to do as much for every customer as possible. This will go a long way towards creating a loyal and satisfied customer base that will return to your store for years to come. Anything less will place the future of your business in trouble.

As an employee of your company you owe it to both your company and the customer to keep each of their best interests at heart and do what is best for everyone. Not what is the cheapest or what is the easiest way out, but what gives everyone involved the best out of the situation. If you do anything less you are doing both your company and your customer a disservice.

Conclusion

As an employee in any company, part of your job is to help the company thrive and grow. You are also expected to adhere to company policies and procedures and to do your job to the best of your abilities. When it comes to customer service that means always doing your best for every customer in every situation.

This job requires creative thinking and sometimes out of the box thinking to arrive at unconventional solutions to unconventional problems. But the good news is that you already have all you need to know to understand each and every customer. Because your customers pretty much want the same things that you and I want. That is because we all are just people at heart.

Not all people are cut out for a career in customer service and that could include you as well. But the reality is that just about anyone who honestly likes people can have a long and successful career in customer service if they will just make the commitment. It requires more common sense than anything else.

It also requires communication skills and the ability to ask questions designed to get to the bottom of things. This is not difficult and it will come to you as you gain experience. Everyone has to start somewhere and that includes you as well. But again, just turn to a co-worker you admire and listen to those little voices in your head and follow their lead. If it sounds good to you it will probably sound good to others as well as long as you are honest with yourself.

So now is the time to go out to your first customer with your newly learned information and put it to use. Start slow and practice until it becomes second nature. Eventually you will be doing all of this without thinking and helping to create the best customer experience possible for each and every customer.

When you reach that point both your customers and your company will thank you for it!

Part Three

Customer Service
All You Have to Know

Consumer Edition

By
David Peters

Disclaimer

Every customer and situation is different so it is not possible to create one universal resolution or approach to any particular customer service issue. Therefore it is up to the individual to evaluate each situation and determine what the proper course of action might be. Some or all parts of this book might not be appropriate for any given situation and it is the responsibility of the reader to determine the proper response and course of action. The writers, publishers, distributors and retailers of this publication assume no responsibility for any or all parts of this book as they might pertain to any specific situation or application.

Introduction

Any time we walk into a store or go online to purchase a product or service, we become a customer. Though that is just common sense, it is important to understand the roles of the business and the customer when it comes to getting the best service and the best possible resolutions to your problems or issues.

Sometimes it helps to understand your role in a certain situation by looking at it through the eyes of the other side. In the case of customer service, that means looking at things from both you point of view and from the customer side of things. That is exactly what we are going to cover in this book so that you can think in those ways throughout any customer service situation.

The issue, or sometimes problem, with customer service is that much of the time the issues are not black and white. In many respects the situations are more gray area than anything else. That means people, both the customer and the business representatives, must be able to think clearly and sometimes go outside the box a bit to come up with a resolution to the situation or problem.

This sometimes requires a bit of negotiation on both sides to arrive at a resolution that is acceptable to both sides. Not everyone gets everything they want in a negotiation. In fact, most of the time there are concessions that should or need to be made. We will go through that process a little later on.

But it is our hope that after reading this book you will have a much better idea of what is involved as both a customer and a business and that this knowledge will help you get better resolutions and better results whenever you have a problem. This could wind up saving you time and money and sometimes a great deal of frustration.

But sometimes even more important, we will show you the thought process you should use BEFORE you make a purchase so that you will get a better all-around experience from whatever it is that you purchase. Because sometimes the decisions you make before you purchase will set the stage for what may happen afterwards. It is better to be safe rather than sorry in many parts of life and customer service is definitely no different.

Please read this book all the way through with an open mind. It might challenge some of the thoughts and ideas that you believe in but at the same time it might give you a few clues as to how you can get more out of the process with a lot less frustration.

Your Role as the Customer

Your role as a customer is very important to every business. Without customers, there is no one to purchase the good or services they offer. Without any sales there is no money to sustain the business and ultimately, after their resources have become depleted, the business will fail. Customer also represent other things to some business as well but providing the revenue and income to the business is the primary reason customers are so valuable.

Your satisfaction is important to the business as well because as a consumer you have choices. Unless the product you are buying is only available from one place (can anyone say "government"?) you will be able to shop around for the best price or overall vale. Because of this businesses must compete for your patronage and ultimately, dollars.

While there are many businesses that do not particularly care whether their customers are happy or not, there are many more that spend a lot of money every year on customer service. They do this to provide better or faster service and to make their customers happy. They realize that this money is well spent because it keeps customers coming back for more time and time again.

Several businesses have built their entire reputations on customer service. Their customers are loyal because they know they will be treated fairly or more than fairly whenever they have a problem of an issue. In fact, this is becoming more and more the case these days as more high-end products are hitting the marketplace. As part of the justification of the high price, they provide exceptional service to their customers.

So right about now you are feeling pretty good about yourself. You now know that you are valuable to the business and that the business really can't stay in business without you and the other customers. So this kind of puts you in the driver's seat. In many cases you can easily say that the business needs you more than you need them. Not in all cases but in most of them. In that respect, it's good to be you.

But since every coin has two sides, there are responsibilities involved in being a customer as well. There are certain things that you must, or at least should, do when it comes to doing business with that company.

Here are a few customer responsibilities every customer needs to be aware of:

Know What You Want

While salespeople are there to assist customers in getting the right products for their needs and applications, they are not there to tell you what you want. Unless you go to a specialty store or service dedicated to providing such information, you should not expect a salesperson to give you certain advice or information.

For example, if you go into a carpet store to buy carpet for your living room, the salesperson will be able to tell you what each type of carpet is made of, what the warranty is, how long it should last and other information because they are trained in that area.

But that same salesperson would not be able to tell you that it will go perfectly with the décor even if you show them a small fuzzy picture on your cell phone. Now if you went to an interior design center and purchased furnishing and carpet together, that is another story because decorating and not just carpet in their area of expertise.

What we are trying to say is that when you walk into a store you should have a pretty good idea of what you want, what you need the product to do and other information such as size, color or other information depending on the product. This is the only way to make even reasonably sure that you get the right product for the application you need.

If you don't provide this information then the salesman might sell you something that will not suit your needs or sell you something that is way more than you need. In either case you will eventually become unhappy and blame the store or the salesperson. So do yourself a favor and take a few moments to think things through and get the right information before you buy and not afterwards. It is a lot easier that way.

Know the Features You Need

An extension of the previous topic, you should understand what you need something to do before you buy it. This will help insure that whatever you do buy will do whatever you need it to without having to pay for features that you don't need. Not everyone needs the ultra-deluxe model with 37 speeds but if you are the one that does need that model, you should be aware of it.

Know Your Budget

Not everyone has a bottomless checkbook and today more and more people are on a budget. Don't be embarrassed by this and make sure the salesperson knows what your budget is. Don't go over your budget unless there is a really, really good reason to do so and even then think twice.

Keep in mind that many salespeople today are working on commission and the higher model you buy the more commission they earn. While a lot of salespeople are honest and trustworthy, some are not. Stay within your budget and if they tell you your budget is too low, go somewhere else and confirm that is indeed the case before you buy.

Pick the Right Company

Whenever there are more than one option as to where to purchase it is up to the consumer to understand the benefits and shortcomings of each dealer before they purchase. That means doing a little research to understand what each store offers their customers. Understanding this now rather than after the sale is always better for the customer.

This means understanding their return policies, their warranty policies, whether or not they charge for delivery, do they service what they sell and several other factors that might add or subtract from the overall value. You can't buy from one store and then demand they honor something that is given by another store. Well, you can, but they are under no obligation to provide it to you.

Understand their Rules and Procedures

Like we just mentioned, different companies might have different policies and procedures that might make a real difference in where you should purchase your products. Ask about all of those things before making a commitment. Understanding this in advance can also give you a little more bargaining leverage as well. For example, if another business offers free delivery and this store doesn't, you might get them to throw in free delivery or reduce the purchase price so that the delivery charge is removed ending up with you getting free delivery.

Provide Accurate Information

I have been in retail for over 40 years and it never ceases to amaze me that people expect salespeople or businesses to automatically know certain things about what they want to purchase. They also expect us to know when they give us false information as well!

For example, if you tell the salesman your other appliances are white, he will sell you a white appliance to match. But if your appliances are ivory and not white and the new one doesn't match, it's not their fault! They acted upon the information you gave them.

If you tell them you have room for a stove that is 36 inches wide and the real opening is 32 inches, it's not going to fit and you will have created all kind of trouble and possibly extra charges for your error. In some cases certain purchases are not refundable and you will be out a lot of money.

Take your time to measure and provide the correct information. Many businesses understand certain common mistakes and may question you but for other information they are at the mercy of whatever you provide them. Take the extra few minutes and confirm what you think is really correct. It will save you time and frustration later.

Treat People Respectfully

As I said I have worked in retail for over 40 years and there is one thing I will tell you that is almost allways100% true. That is that you will get more from other people and businesses if you treat them with respect.

This does not mean that you cannot argue with them or disagree with what they tell you. But there are right ways to get your point across and there are wrong ways. Being rude or abusive or using foul language is not the way to get someone to help you. Using those tactics or approaches is the best way to be shut down and asked to leave.

For me personally, I always tried to do more for the person who was reasonable and respectful.

In one particular case I had to turn down someone's request because they had damaged the product themselves and it was not a defect. They understood that and thanked me for their time. The next person was a raving and screaming lunatic who was very obnoxious and rude to me as well. After getting done talking to that customer, I called the nice one back and told her that because she was so nice I would give her a new product at no charge.

It does pay to be nice and treat people with respect. Don't let them walk all over you but treat them with respect.

Be Reasonable

As a customer, you are entitled to fair and reasonable treatment and resolution by the business. The two key words in that sentence are "Fair" and "Reasonable". Unfortunately, some customer seem to think that as long as they feel what they want is reasonable then that is fair. The problem with that is that not all customer expectations are reasonable.

Over the years I have seen some really outlandish demands and expectations from many different customers.

From a customer who refused to pay a $25,000 bill because a $5 piece was missing from her order to another customer who demanded that she get her entire house repainted because the sides that were in the shade looked different than the sides that were in full sunlight!

Your demands as a customer should be reasonable in respect to the situation. If you purchase a product that appears to be defective you should be entitled to a new one or a full refund possibly including shipping charges. But if the product didn't damage anything or hurt someone you should not be demanding $5,000 in pain and suffering because the pair of pants you purchased had the wrong size label on them.

We will discuss customer demands in more detail in future chapters. But for now, let's just say that your demands should be fair and within reason as compared to the product and situation involved. Anything more is likely to not only get turned down but cause you to get less in the long run.

Be Realistic

When it comes to the products we choose or the demands we make or even our expectations we have we need to be realistic. No product lasts forever so we shouldn't expect it to. No one is perfect, including ourselves so we shouldn't expect others to be perfect either. There are limits to how low a price can go and there are limits to concessions people can make as well.

What I mean is do not expect a salesperson to throw in $200 worth of free items so you will buy a $100 product. That is not being realistic. Do not call in a complaint and demand a call back within 5 minutes or you are calling your attorney. Trust me when I say these are actual examples that I have encountered and they didn't end like the customer had hoped!

Be Educated

When I say "be educated" I am not referring to getting a college degree or a doctorate. The knowledge I am referring to is being knowledgeable when it comes to what you are buying and where you are buying it from. This is the basis of the old saying "Let the buyer beware!"

Before you go out to buy something, do a bit of research into the product so you get to know a little bit about it. This is especially true when there are difficult models or brands to choose from. While a salesman can help you, it is ultimately your responsibility to make sure you get what you need and want. Plus, a little bit of knowledge can help you see through a phony sales pitch or sales techniques.

With the arrival of the internet doing research is easier than ever before. Go to a few websites and see what's available and what the prices are. This way when you walk into a store you will know what to expect and can easily spot a great price or a phony "sale" price. You can always use this knowledge to gain leverage in the sales process as well.

Another important reason to be knowledgeable is that people tend to treat knowledgeable people differently. While an uneducated customer might be identified as "an easy mark" for an aggressive salesperson, an educated customer usually gets less hype and less sales pressure. So not only will you know more about what you are thinking about buying but you will be treated better throughout the sales process as well.

As far as all customer service interaction is concerned, perhaps the best thing you can do for yourself is to know as much as you can about the product and the business before you buy. This way your interests will be protected.

At this point you understand your leverage as a customer and also the responsibilities that come with being a customer. While a lot of this is common sense, you would be shocked to see how many customers fail to grasp these simple concepts. Spend just one afternoon behind a customer service desk or on a customer service phone and you will quickly see that this is true.

So now that you are an informed customer and aware of your leverage and rights, let's take a look at things from the other point of view because it is important that you understand that as well.

The Company Side
of Customer Service

As a customer you might feel that how the company feels about customer service is none of your concern. If you do feel that way let me say that unfortunately, you are 100% wrong. The fact is, there are also aspects of the customer service process that must be understood from the company's point of view as well. Being able to do so will allow you to get more out of the process with less frustration and aggravation.

First of all, we have already discussed how the company needs people like you and I as customers which gives us leverage over the business when it comes to resolving problems. But another side of the coin exists as well. We need the business as well if we are to have someplace to go in the future for more products and/ or service. So the bottom line is that both customers and businesses need each other. Which need is greater, business or customer, will depend on several factors.

But the important thing to realize that if the business ceases to be profitable it will soon cease to exist. Contrary to what you might hear from labor unions and other spokespeople, the public will only pay so much for a product or service and once that price is exceeded the customer will no longer buy it. So there is a limit on income and if there are to be profits generated then there has to be a limit on expenses as well.

Since customer service is an expense, and since resolving problems costs time and money, every business is limited to what they can or are willing to do in order to make a customer happy. This does not mean they don't want to make you happy. It just means that they cannot afford to at times. If a business were to give every customer everything they wanted, customers would love them but they would eventually go out of business.

What this means is that businesses must have rules and policies in place that not only protect the customer but also protect the business as well. Policies such as a 30 day return policy instead of unlimited returns or a one year warranty instead of a lifetime warranty. Limits are put in place to ensure the long-term survival of the business and for those who provide the products and services to those businesses.

One of the rule of customer service as far as companies are concerned is that the customer doesn't give a darn about their rules, policies or procedures. But the fact is, the customer needs to understand the reasons behind these and understand that those same rules are there for the good of everyone. Because of this we should not look at policies and procedures as unfair or unreasonable. How we should look at them is as to whether or not they are fair or not.

For example, if I purchase an automobile, I would expect a multi-year warranty because of the high price of the vehicle. The warranty should reflect pretty much the industry standard. So let's say that warranty is 3 year parts and labor. Anything more is great while anything less would be considered negative. Unless there are really unique or special circumstance, there are not refunds or exchanges for the same reasons.

Those polices are fair and equitable for both the consumer and the business. They protect both parties equally.

But If I were to purchase a cordless phone for $50 I would get a 90 day one-year warranty and probably a 30 day return policy. Both are long enough to make sure the product is free of defects and that it is suitable for our purposes or application. To expect a 3 year warranty would be unusual. To not be able to return or exchange it would be unacceptable as well.

We also need to understand that every solution to a problem is going to cost a business money. They understand this and those funds are built into the prices and their business model. So it is not that they are looking to run away from their obligations. They seek only to limit them to fair and reasonable levels.

For example, if you that cordless phone you purchased had a 90 days warranty and it stopped working in 120 days, the business might consider replacing it because it would cost them less than $50 to do so and it would keep a customer happy. Plus, they could probably return it for credit anyway. That would be a reasonable solution cost-wise for the business.

But if you had troubles with your car and the 3 year warranty ran out you would not likely be offered a new car free of charge because that would cost the dealer too much. You might be able to negotiate a free or discounted repair though because that is more cost-effective for the dealer.

While you don't have to agree with this philosophy it is important to understand it. Because once you understand it and try to work within the system you can open up a lot of alternatives that could very well give you a lot more of what you want from the business.

This is because there are two ways to resolve a customer service situation and one is often a lot more appealing to the business than the other.

The first way is to give a refund, repair the product or a new product. Sometimes this is a no-brainer and the easiest way to resolve a problem of a dispute. If something fails within the warranty period and there is no repair option then a refund or new product is given. This is usually the case with low cost products or with any product that cannot be repaired and is proven defective.

The business, in these cases, returns the product to the manufacturer for a credit so the only loss to the business is the mark-up charged to the customer if a refund is given. If a new product was provided it costs the business only the labor cost to return the product and process the paperwork. So the exposure to the business is fairly limited and most businesses will not hesitate to go this route as long as the defective is confirmed.

If the product can be repaired the business will process this or direct the customer as to how to get their products repaired. Again this is cost-effective for the business even if they do the repair themselves because they are compensated by the manufacturer. The end result is that the business gets the issue resolve economically and the customer gets their product repaired free of charge.

The second way is a little bit different and requires a little creative thinking on behalf of the customer and the business. That is because there are way to give a customer more of what they want without incurring much of a cost. And that is by providing them with alternate items of a certain perceived value that really cost the business very little. Providing items such as these can give the customer a great value at little or no cost to the business.

Let's say the business normally charges for delivery of an appliance. They might provide you with free delivery on your next purchase which might save you $50 but cost the business almost nothing. Or maybe they offer to perform a free maintenance on your product. This might be normally worth $100 but cost the business just an hour of a technician's time which might only cost them $25 or even less during the slow time of the year when they are looking for work.

Whatever the item being offered might be the main point of providing or requesting these things is that it represents a way for a business to make a customer happy for a fraction of the cost of a refund or new product.

A perfect example of this happened to me when we went to a famous theme park and the management there messed up our ticket order costing us about an hour to resolve. To help make us happy they sent us four 7-day passes good for the next year! These were worth approx. $700 at the time which made me very happy!

But the actual cost to the theme park was the cost of printing the tickets which was probably less than 25 cents! That 25 cents it cost them was worth over $700 to me which was great for both of us. Plus we went again the next year and stayed at the theme park and bought their food as well. So not only was I thrilled they got even more of our money!

Using these value-added extras is one great way to use your understanding of customer service from the business point of view and use it to your advantage. If your demands are refused, or if you see that they want to help you but can't try and come up with one or two of these other options and you might walk away from the situation with everyone being very happy.

Keep in mind that the business might not offer these to you for a couple of reasons. First of all the employee might not be aware that they can do this sort of thing or they might not be accustomed to thinking in that manner. Or, despite the low cost they might not be willing volunteer the offer unless they have to.

But if you understand how business works and why they do what they do you can often use that knowledge to get more of what you want out of the situation. You have nothing to lose for trying and as long as you don't go overboard and demand too much you will probably find everyone very receptive to your suggestions.

Remember as you move forward through any customer service process that there are limits to what business and individuals are going to do to help you no matter how much you push or even threaten. But if you understand the reasons behind the rules and how you might be able to work around them you will find the entire process much easier.

Being Fair

In all the year I worked in retail and in business I have found that an overwhelming majority of people working in the customer service field have an honest desire to help people. It takes a special kind of person to work in customer service day in and day out because the very nature of the job can be very negative depending on your job function.

For the people who provide information and handling administrative manner sometimes the volume becomes so high the stress level goes crazy. For those who are in charge of handling complaints or resolving issues there can be an overwhelming negativity because of the constant negative situations they are exposed to.

But regardless of whatever position these people had, all they wanted to do is help people and be fair when it came to their problems and what they could do to help them. Unfortunately not all customers felt the same way and constantly confronted these people with outrageous demands and threats. Not only did this usually not get the result that the customer wanted, they usually got less than what they might have received.

The best way to resolve any problem is to try to be fair about the entire process. You should understand, however, that sometimes the customer's definition of "fair" might be totally different" than the employees. While this does not always mean that either party is wrong, it just makes it more difficult to resolve any situation when one or both people are not trying to be fair.

This also applies to the entire sales process as well. Do not expect a salesperson to sell you a $300 television for $29.95. If you make that demand you will pretty much shut down the desire of the salesperson to help you because he sees you as being too unrealistic and your expectations too high. The same goes for other demands as well. Ask for what you want but make your request reasonable.

There is a philosophy related to negotiation that says you should start out asking for the moon and then give back as you gain more concessions from the other person. While this is effective you should not start out so high that you "turn off" the other person. That is just counter-productive and will not get you anywhere. Ask for a little bit more than you expect so you do have some negotiation room. Who knows, you just might get what you want or you might have to give back a little.

But this needs to work both ways as well. The business needs to treat you fairly as well. To be honest there are businesses out there that abandon their customer once they have their money and you walk out the door. This is exactly why we talked about doing your research as to where to buy your products.

Doing business with companies that treat their customers fairly just makes the entire process go faster easier and less stressful. Sometimes this is worth a lot more than saving 29 cents off the purchase price. In other words, cheaper isn't always better.

Your end goal is to be thought of as someone who is willing to work towards a resolution and not someone who is perceived to be overly demanding and impossible to please. Believe me when I say people will work harder and longer for someone they perceive as trying to do the right thing than they are trying to make a demanding jerk happy. It's just human nature.

When You Have a Problem

Sometimes the best intentions on both sides are not enough to come to a satisfactory resolution. This might be because the demands exceed the authority of the people involved or because of a disagreement as to what is covered or who is to blame. Whenever these situations do occur how we handle them can make all the difference in the world.

Here are some things to consider when trying to resolve a situation that you are having trouble with:

Don't Yell

Sometimes people have the reaction to start yelling the minute something doesn't go the way they want or whenever they are told they are not going to get something they want.

While this might be a natural reaction, it is non-productive especially at the beginning or early stages of the conflict.

Talking more loudly or yelling tends to escalate the negativity of any situation. As tempers rise and emotions flare the ability to communicate effectively and not with our emotions becomes a lot more difficult. The angrier we get the more our emotions take over. So keep your emotions in check and your voice at a normal level.

Don't Threaten

I live in an area where the first words out of a customer's mouth are "I'm going to call my lawyer!" whenever they don't get exactly what they want. This doesn't work for a few reasons. First of all, the vast majority of people who threaten to call their lawyer never do. It is an empty threat. Businesses know this. I mean, does it really make sense to get a lawyer involved and pay a few hundred dollars to solve a $29.95 problem? No it doesn't.

The same applies for people who threaten to write letter after letter to all kind of consumer groups and agencies. Though more people will actually do this that will call their lawyer, it is still a relatively small number of people and businesses understand this.

But perhaps the main reason for not threatening is that once you make a threat the company might resort to the minimum that they need to do under the law.

If your warranty is a 90 day warranty and it is day 91, threaten and you are going to be held to the 90 days. Be nice and you might get a new product or something else.

Threatening at the beginning of the process, before you have exhausted all the standard options and gone through the process is just an unnecessary and premature action that could have negative consequences. Your best option at this point is to escalate the situation to a manager or someone higher up in the company that will hopefully have the authority to grant your requests. Or, if that isn't an option look for alternate solutions at the level you currently are at.

Don't Make a Scene

Some people love to make a scene. They love to yell and scream and make a fuss thinking that the business will not want to risk other customers hearing what is going on and just grant your wishes. Unfortunately, that doesn't usually work and when it does work, it can work against you.

It might result in you being made to look bad in front of other people and if the case should escalate to law enforcement or a trial you will now have witnesses against you. This is especially damaging if the other person is honestly trying to help and you are just ranting about anything and everything.

Your best bet is to remain calm and talk to people hopefully in private. Talking in private is much better because not only will there be no witnesses but employees and managers are more likely to grant concessions or do more in private because they can do so without anyone else knowing. The thought here is that they can give you something extra without anyone else finding out and setting a bad precedent.

Talking in private is also better because some people, once they become aware that others are watching, become afraid to back down and appear weak in front of others. So this can result in someone sticking to their argument or demands even though they realize they are foolish or irresponsible. Sometimes pride just gets in the way so try and avoid that if at all possible.

Plus, acting calm and talking in private makes it less likely that the issue will get heated and more difficult to resolve. So don't make a scene and instead concentrate on resolving the problem.

Act Positive

When you are trying to resolve a problem try using only positive words. Hearing a negative word make our brains shut down and sometimes prevents us from hearing whatever is coming next. So instead of saying no to an offer instead thank them for the offer and make a counter-offer.

Every statement you make and every word should be focused on making the situation better. Do not dwell on what cannot be done. Instead, think of things that can be done and how they can help resolve the matter. Complaining on and on about what cannot happen doesn't do anyone any good and does not lead to any kind of positive resolution.

Do Know What You Want

If you are in a dispute or disagreement with someone, understand in advance what it is you want and why you want it. The last thing you want to do is get what you asked for and then realize that is not going to solve the problem. Think things through in advance and make sure what you are asking for is what you really want. Once you make the demands it is very difficult to take them back or then ask for something more.

Do Have Options in Mind

Sometimes the best solution to a problem is not a straight line. Maybe they cannot give you what you want exactly like you want it. So maybe we have to look for alternative methods or solutions that will get you where you need to be.

We already discussed value-added extras or solutions and these should be on the table as well. The more choices we have to come up with a satisfactory resolution the easier and less stressful it is going to be on everyone involved.

Use Precedents to Your Advantage

If someone else you know had the same problems and received a certain resolution from the same company and it is something you would like as well, bring it up to the company and ask if you can get the same offer. Chances are if they gave it to one person they will give it to you as well. The exception might be if the situation was significantly different in your case.

Initial Escalation

Sometimes your best efforts are just not going to be enough and you are going to have to go to the next level. I am not talking about yelling or going legal or anything like that. At least not at this point. But you should understand that the person you are talking with might not have the authority to do what you want or grant your requests.

Though employees should recognize this first and escalate the situation on their own they might be under instructions not to do so unless the customer asks. So in a nice and calm voice, thank them for their time and nicely ask if you can speak to their manager or someone higher up in the company.

If that person is not available for some reason, ask for their contact information so you can talk to them later.

The whole idea with escalation is that you will be dealing with someone with more authority and power in the company. Very often these individuals will see things in a different perspective and very well could see the value in giving you what you asked for.

That is because managers or owners see this situation as just not one sale but instead see this situation as part of your entire history as a customer in the company. When they do this your value to the company increases and it might make sense to go a little bit higher when it comes to making you happy. This is all a difference in perspective and having someone else see a higher value in retaining you as a customer.

Escalation also helps reduce tensions and emotions as well.

Keep Detailed Records & Names

Throughout the process it is important to keep track of who you talked to and when and how you talked to them as well. If it was via e-mail make sure you save and make copies of the e-mails. If it was an in-person visit the record the date and time and any others that might be present. If it was a phone conversation record the date and time as well.

You might think that some or possibly all of this is not required but remember that sometimes these situations cannot be resolved locally and you might have to have proof of what has already taken place should this turn into a legal issue of if you should decide to make a complaint to the Better Business Bureau or Consumer Affairs.

Whenever you file any kind of complaint they are going to want a history or account of what has taken place to date. Having a written record allows you to put together a timeline that is accurate and complete. Trying to remember things after the fact days or weeks later can result in inaccurate or incomplete information. Whenever there is a mistake on your part there are chances that the rest of your information, no matter how accurate, might also be brought into questions by others.

Keeping Things Local

Though some might disagree on this particular point, I greatly prefer keeping the dispute local as long as I have even the slightest feeling that people want to help me. This is because the higher up you go or the more complaints that you file, the fewer options might be open to the local people who really want to try and help you.

For example, maybe you are just out of warranty on a product but a local customer service rep offers to replace the product under warranty as a courtesy to you.

If you make other demands which they are unwilling to meet and you escalate the issue or file a complaint, the issue might be taken away from the local people and you not only might not have your demands met but you might lose the product replacement offer as well. This is something you should think seriously about. There are times to file complaints and then there are times to accept your losses and take what the company offers you especially if it above what they are obligated to do.

Thank People

Even though you might not resolve the situation, or the situation might have been resolved in a way that you are not happy with, still take the time to thank the people involved who were trying to help resolve your problem. Most people do not take this step when things don't go there way and it can wind up hurting them down the road.

Leaving people with a positive comment might soften their position or feelings down the road as they remember you as a nice person with some compassion. Is this going to happen all the time? Well, no, but you have little to lose and potentially a lot to gain.

The one thing you do not want to do is bring yourself down to a lower level by being rude or discourteous. We discussed the reasons for not doing that earlier and the higher up you get in the process the more this will hold true. Always keep your dignity and reputation intact when dealing with anyone regardless of how they might be treating you. It is better to walk away than to resort to unflattering behavior.

Escalation

In those cases where all efforts have been exhausted and a satisfactory settlement is not possible, you have a decision to make. You either abandon the situation and chalk it up to experience or you can attempt to escalate the matter either further up in the company or get outside agencies or resources involved. There is no one perfect choice or answer and what you should do will depend on your particular situation.

I will say this, however. Before filing complaints or contacting lawyers sit down and go over the situation again to make sure what you are seeking is reasonable and appropriate. This is important because once you file a complaint or contact a lawyer the entire matter ratchets up a whole other level and there will be additional time and resources required to follow through.

If, after careful thought and weighing of the options you decide to accept a previous offer by all means go back and see if that offers is still available.

As long as you have been fair and just up to this point you will probably find that it is. If that is the case then go and accept it and close the matter completely.

But if you find that even after thinking it over completely, and possibly running it by someone else as well, that you are really entitled to more than what is being offered you should then take the next step and escalate the issue.

Here are some of the most common ways or escalating a problem or situation:

To the Owner or CEO

Sometimes if you are dealing with a larger company where you cannot meet with the owner in person as part of a routine escalation you can write a letter to the owner or CEO informing them of your problem. Here's why this can be very effective:

In large companies the CEO does not usually red these letters themselves but instead they employ people to read and act upon these letters. Their job is to resolve the complaints or at least confirm their merit with the objective of never reaching the desk of the CEO.

This is important because the person or people in charge of reading and processing these letters want to keep as many of them off the CEO's desk as possible. They regard every complaint that has merit but isn't resolved to be a defeat of sorts and they will often go to great lengths to make sure that doesn't happen.

This does not mean that your complaint doesn't have to be valid because it does. What is likely going to happen is that they will reach out to local employees who were handling this or employees located in your area and ask them to get involved. They will usually be given parameters within which they can act to resolve the issue. In most cases you will get more of what you asked for in this approach.

Though phone calls might work as well for the same reasons, I believe a letter, or possibly an e-mail will be a better alternative. E-Mails can be especially effective in that they have a time and date stamp on them so they can never claim they didn't receive your e-mail. But often times you will not have the e-mail address required and instead will have to use the generic e-mail address listed on the website. If that is the case with you I suggest sending the e-mail and following it up with a letter to make sure the right people see it and red it.

To the Better Business Bureau

Contacting the Better Business Bureau is sometimes thought of as being the "old school" approach but sometimes the old ways are still the best. The great thing about the Better Business Bureau is that companies take their inquiries and complaints seriously.

That is because whenever someone calls the BBB and inquiries about open complaints, they are given the number of complaints and unresolved complaints.

The last thing a company wants is to have customers turn away from their company because of what they perceive are a lot of negative complaints. Since the BBB is still one of the first place people go to check out a company, complaints listed there can carry considerable weight.

But keep in mind that the BBB investigates complaints and does not just take your word for what happened. Everything is checked out, your story compared with the company's version and if it is determined that the complaint has merit they will encourage both sides to resolve the dispute. Having the BBB on your side gives you more leverage and gives the company more reason to settle than continue to drag things out.

To Local Consumer Affairs

Local Consumer Affairs office are another alternative but sometimes they lack the same effect on businesses as the BBB might. But one very important role of the Consumer Affairs Office that might have significant weight is their ability to take legal action on your behalf and even rescind or suspend a company's license to do business in the area.

You can contact your local office and have them send you the required forms or where you can download them.

Then you would fill out the forms and follow their processes. Keep in mind that your area might have both a local and state office that you can contact.

The same warnings apply as with other forms of escalation that everything is checked and verified so do not try to lie or spin the facts in order to make your position stronger. This can come back to haunt you in the process.

The State Attorney General's Office

If there were laws broken or if you did not receive the proper treatment under the terms of a warranty or other specific matter, reporting this to the State Attorney General's Office might be an effective way to go.

If this office finds a law has been broken or that you were treated unfairly they can bring charges against the company for doing so. When this is a possibility the company will often do anything you want to make sure that doesn't happen.

I had purchased a computer from a well-known company and had constant problems with it and their support accomplished nothing. Neither did my e-mails and letters. But one complaint to the State Attorney General and they sent me a brand new computer at no cost. So this approach can work. It is especially effective if the product has a well-known problem or defect.

Forums, Message Boards & Internet Comments

While I am not a huge fan of bulletin boards and forums, they can be effective in getting your message out to the public if the right people see your post or message. And that is where the problem often comes in.

Many, if not most, people who post on bulletin boards or forums post negative comments. While some of them are true others might be exaggerations of the truth or outright lies due to someone else's own personal agenda. Contrary to popular belief not everything you see, hear or read on the internet is true.

The difference in posting or printing on these venues is that they are read by the public. Because of this if you publish false claims or information about a person or a business, or if you misrepresent the facts in any way people can sue you for slander. So make very sure what you write or post is 100% accurate and that you have the documentation and information to back up wrote you write. Otherwise you can be causing yourself even more trouble than what you have now.

Newspapers & Media

This category is interesting because it primarily deals with radio, television and print media outlets. Get a popular story on all of these media outlets and you might reach a HUGE audience. But the problem is getting the exposure in the first place.

Channel 21 is not going to broadcast a story about you not getting your 2 year MP3 player replaced for free because it broke. There is just not enough interested to justify running the story. But if your story is similar to the stories of many other people, you might have a chance.

The more people that have the same or similar stories, the better the chance of getting your story told. The more trouble the company is in might help as well. But generally speaking, breaking through to these outlets is quite difficult.

The exception to this are news shows that have a "Problem Solver" or other similar segment where they put an investigative reporter on your story and try to resolve it. If you can get on one of those segments, you might not have much trouble getting most or all of what you want. Companies will do a lot more in order to avoid negative publicity on radio and television than most other forms of media.

Legal

We will be discussing this in more detail in the next chapter but for now, lets it suffice to say that going the legal route is usually reserved for the last resort. Unless there is damage or injury involved the costs might outweigh the judgement on these types of cases. But again, more of this shortly.

Bluffing

Some people just write up the complaints and send copies of them to the company without actually submitting the paperwork or filing the actual complaint. The idea is that the company thinks you are sending in the complaints to the stated organizations and then tries to resolve it before the agencies contact them. It is an interesting ploy that sometimes works quite well.

In other cases, especially when the demands or cost to settle is relatively high, the will wait for the actual complaint to be filed and then try to settle at that point. In these cases it is the company and the customer trying to see who folds first.

I strongly urge everyone to try and get issues resolved without burdening these already overworked agencies. While they are there to help support and protect people, they should not be handling frivolous complaints or bogus ones. And for the opinion that these people are there because you are paying taxes, that still does not give you the right to file frivolous complaints or claims.

Keep in mind that contacting these people or agencies is just the first step. After they contact you there will still be negotiations that will take place to see how your particular situation or problem is resolved. If you are reasonable the chances of getting a satisfactory results will be much greater.

But if the reason you couldn't resolve it in the beginning was because your demands or requirements were very excessive, chances are you will leave this phase of the process with the same result.

Again, as you go through this part of the process write down every detail such as who contacted who by what method and on what date and what the reason for the correspondence was at that point in time. Include names and addresses in case this information is needed in the future should things get escalated even higher.

Wording Your Complaint or Letter

Writing a letter of complaint is not like writing a letter to a friend or relative. The person or people reading these letters usually have many to go through so they do not have a lot of time to read each one. With that in mind here are a few suggestions to follow as you prepare your letter:

Be Brief

Keep your letter to one page whenever possible. Give as much detail as needed but not too much more. You want people to get the important information that really matters. Keep opinions and fluff to a minimum. In other words, get to the point, make your point and finish as quickly as possible.

Write it Well

Don't write a letter full of errors and misspellings.

Use proper grammar and make it sound as professional as possible. After you write it read it back aloud to make sure it flows well. Rewrite the weaker parts and make it sound compelling.

Use Facts

Include as much specific information as possible. That means specific names, dates, facts and other specific information that helps you make your case and give the person reading your letter the background they need in order to know how to proceed. The more facts you use the better. Remember you want to drive home your message clearly and accurately and nothing accomplishes this more than facts and specifics.

Make it Positive

Don't complain in your letter or tell the reader how annoying the employee was that handled your problem. Instead, keep it as positive as possible telling them you know they will do the right thing and resolve this problem because you are a patient and long-time customer. At this point do not make any threats. Wait for them to turn down you request or worse, not respond at all. For right now you want to write a positive letter designed to create a positive impression that will get positive results.

Be Polite

Use calm language and be polite. No four letter words or mean spirited text. You want people to want to help you not grow to despise you as they read your letter. The old saying "You get more flies with sugar" certainly applies here.

Sending the Letter

I prefer sending all correspondence certified or at least with a return receipt so you have proof that it was received. This keeps the company from saying they never received any correspondence from you. This can help if the problem takes a legal route.

You might not be able to do that if the only mailing address is a PO Box as those cannot have receipts given because there is no one to sign for them. In those cases, if you cannot find an alternative address, then send it regular mail and give it time for a response. If none is forthcoming mail it again.

If you have an e-mail address for the person or company you can send it there as well. Just don't delete it from your sent file should you need it later. You can always print out a copy and keep it in your files in case you need it.

Legal Issues

For some this is the last resort while for others it might be the first resort. As I said before, unless there is injury or property damage involved you are almost always better off trying to resolve it in other ways than running to court. Even small claims courts have fees and then there is the inconvenience as well to consider.

But if you are sure it will be worth your while to not accept any offer made so far and take this to court, here are a few things you should be aware of before making that decision:

Cost

Though these will vary from state to state and town to town, be aware that there will be filing fees and other fees that will have to be paid before your case will be scheduled. You can get a schedule of fees from your attorney or your local courts if you are not using an attorney.

But also be aware that an attorney may be required for certain types of cases depending on local laws and statutes. Be sure to know these rules and understand them before filings the paperwork. Naturally if a lawyer is required that will greatly increase the cost of bringing this matter to trial.

Make sure you weight the costs against the potential benefits to see if it is really a good idea to file suit. Sometimes it just makes sense to set principles aside and save a bunch of money by just letting the matter go. But that is your decision.

An alternative to actually filing a lawsuit might be to hire an attorney to write a letter to the company on your behalf letting them know of your intention to file a lawsuit. Sometimes just this little extra push has been known to result in a satisfactory settlement. If this doesn't happen with you, you can always file an actual suit later on.

Time Frame

Depending on where you live you might have to wait months or even years to have your matter brought up in the courts. Keep in mind that the other company is likely to do its best to stall things for as long as possible hoping that you will just give up and go away. So be prepared to show up at court only to hear that a postponement was granted. This is all part of the games that companies often play.

Keep in mind that throughout this delay your situation is placed on hold and you will not be allowed to take certain action until the case has been heard. This might mean having to hold on to the product paying any licensing, storage free or other expenses as you go along and other matters. Be sure to factor this in as well when deciding if this is something worth pursuing.

Legal Requirements

The legal system is a very involved and complex system. There are all kinds of loopholes and special wording and actions that must be taken in certain orders and all kinds of other things you have to be worried about.

Even if you are acting as your own attorney in small claims court, it is wise to at least consult with an attorney to make sure you are doing everything as you should be. Otherwise you run the risk of having your case thrown out on a technicality and having to start all over again and paying another set of fees in the process.

Your Rights as a Consumer

I am going to say this with every intention not to be cynical. While I believe in the legal system it doesn't always work as it should when it comes to being fair to all parties.

Before you file your suit make sure you have legal standing to do so. Just because something is right does not make it legal.

For example, you might have a legitimate problem after owning a product for 100 days. You might be 100% correct that the product is defective. But if you have a90 day guarantee and file your lawsuit on the 100th day, you might be out of luck.

Very little in trials involves judgment or common sense. Instead it is whether or not something meets a certain legal definition or not. If your claims meet the legal definition you win. If they don't you lose. It can be simple as that. Do not take someone to court based on principles because while that might give you a sense of right it will not give you a victory in court.

Submit Your Case Clearly and Factually

If you are acting as your own lawyer than present your case to the judge clearly and accurately without theatrics. Stick to how your rights were violated or which laws or statues the company failed to comply with in how they treated you. Use as many facts as possible and refrain from making your own judgments or condemning the company.

If you prepare your case carefully and have specific legal precedents and facts behind you it should be easy for you to emerge victorious. If you don't have any legal basis or fats to support your case you probably should not have filed it in the first place.

After the Dispute is Over

After the dispute is over you should document the final resolution and then follow-up to make sure everything that was promised was delivered. This is important because sometimes things fall through the cracks and something gets missed or forgotten.

This is especially important when a legal judgment is involved because sometimes a company will refuse to follow the findings of the court or delay things to avoid doing what it was ordered to do. In some cases you may have to go back to court. Either way, make sure you get what was ordered by the court and that you get it within the time frame promised.

Another possibility is that the company might appeal the decision especially if there were injuries or damages and the judgment was very costly.

If this happens it is important that you continue to document everything that happens and make copies of every communication you receive about the matter. This will help you throughout the appeal process as well as provide you with added information that might be of use moving forward.

But for most of us, we will not have to go to court and fight any of those battle. Instead we will just get what we were promised in the final resolution and move on. Most of the time if our complaints are valid we will get some kind of restitution or resolution. It might not be exactly what we wanted but we will get something. Hopefully the final outcome was a positive one for you.

I have always thought it a good idea to end these processes on a positive note. That means thanking the people who helped you even though it might have been a bit confrontational at times. You might go as far as writing a letter to the owner of the company thanking them and their employees for taking care of a loyal customer. Of course, you would only write that if the outcome was a positive one.

But sometimes the outcome is not positive for whatever reason. Maybe it was determined that your complaint had no merit or maybe the company was just very determined not to give you a thing for whatever reason and it wasn't worth it to escalate it to a legal battle. These things happen and we need to just learn from the experience and move on in life. Hopefully at least the lessons learned will help us moving forward.

Some people might be tempted to keep on complaining and writing letters and posting comments and this is within your rights to do so as long as what you write is accurate and factual and does not fall under the act of harassment. The last thing you want to do is find yourself in legal trouble because of a letter or posting you made.

If you do continue your letter writing, follow the same protocol discussed in this book. Keep your letters non-confrontational and state the facts as you see them. It is always possible that someone different might see your letter and take some action on your behalf. But the fact really is that the more letters you write the less likely they are to be read. But there is always the chance.

Instead, if there are other places to purchase the products you need then perhaps you should check those businesses out and start doing business with them. This is perhaps the biggest weapon you have as far as responding to how you were treated in the past. If a company treats their customers poorly and they leave and go elsewhere eventually that is going to be noticed in their declining sales. Nothing hits a business harder than lost revenue. Some people even publicize the treatment they received in hopes of driving others away as well. This can be effective as well and might help you get a settlement just to get you to stop.

But again, if you are going to adopt such a response make sure that it is 100% true and factual. Not 90% or even 99% true. The business will jump on action false statements and you could find yourself in real trouble. Always keep in mind that businesses, especially larger ones, have a lot more money available to fight legal issues than you or I. That might not be fair but it is the reality of the situation.

But perhaps the best attitude to take is one that will help you stay out of these situations moving forward. Here are a few things you can do to minimize the chances of finding yourself in an on-going dispute:

Research the Company

Buy only from companies that have a proven track record for good customer treatment. This becomes more important as the cost of the product increases. After all, it is easier to go out and buy a new loaf of bread for $2 than it is to try and return a $2,500 defective sound system!

Check the company for complaints with the Better Business Bureau and your local Office of Consumer Affairs. If there are a lot of complaints, look to go somewhere else. If the company is "clean" that's a good sign.

Also go on various websites and forums to see if there are any bad comments about them.

Search under the company name to see what is out there online. But keep in mind that not everything you read on the internet is true and there are a lot of people who post bad comments that are false and a lot of companies who will post phony positive comments to make them appear better than they really are.

After all the research determine if the company is someplace you would like to do business with. If you have other options, investigate them. If there are no other options then go into the process with your eyes open and ask a ton of questions and make sure everything is in writing that needs to be.

Research the Product

The best way to get the best product is to do your research before you buy. Do the same things you did researching the company but do it for the product you are considering purchasing. Look at reviews and consumer comments to see how others feel about the product after they actually used it. Just because sales literature or a salesman says a product is really good doesn't make it so!

Be Suspicious

Our parents used to tell us that it is always a good idea to give someone the benefit of the doubt.

This means you should try and take things at face value unless there is strong evidence that you shouldn't. But the problem is our parents and grandparents did not grow up in the world we live in today. There are more scammers and cheats out there today than ever before and there will be even more tomorrow.

Though it is a hard way to go through life, I approach everything and everyone I have encountered for the first time with a healthy dose or suspicion. Then I let the situation proceed until I am confident that everything is like it should be. I wouldn't blindly give someone my life savings to invest without a thorough investigation into their background just because they "looked nice" and I wouldn't make a large purchase either without doing my homeowner first.

Don't get me wrong though. The vast majority of people in this world are upstanding and honest people and those are who you will usually interact with in life. But you cannot ignore the others who will do anything to take advantage of you and take what is yours. Because you know they exist it would be irresponsible to ignore their presence.

If It Looks too Good….

Sometimes we look back after something bad happened and we see how foolish we were in believing something that was told us or shown us.

What we thought was an absolutely amazing once in a life time offer turned out to be a scam. We should have realized it but we found ourselves blinded by dreams or perhaps greed.

Scammers and cheats prey on our emotions and our greed. They promise us something wonderful and in our minds we see a better or richer life and we are hooked. These people have refined their approach and methods so well just about everyone is a target for them.

If someone presents you with a deal or offer that appears too good to be true, it probably isn't true. If everyone is selling something for $500 and someone tells you they can sell it to you for $100, then watch out. Something isn't right.

Just look at the people who have lost their life savings to financial schemes. Had they stopped to think that everyone else was paying 3% on investments but these people were promising 15%, they would have realized something fishy was going on. But again, greed plays tricks on us and we often hope against hope for a better life or more money.

If it looks too good to be true, run like hell in the opposite direction.

For more information on Customer Service please visit our website at:

http://www.allyouhavetoknow.com

(New website available in November of 2015)

Or visit the website of
The Customer Service Training Institute at

http://www.infowhse.com

Tips for Best Handling Consumer Problems

If you have a problem or complaint, do not wait to file it. There might be deadlines or time frames involved that could help or hurt you case. Don't put it off. File it as soon as you can.

If you have to go into a store to deal with an issue, bring your spouse or a friend with you. You are likely to be treated better when there are witnesses around. Plus, the other person can confirm or deny what was said during the interaction.

Whenever possible, put things and get things in writing. A letter or an e-mail is a permanent record that cannot be denied. But people can very easily deny saying anything they supposedly said.

Keep your demands reasonable. Do not demand the moon with the idea of accepting less. This can backfire on you. Ask for a bit more so you will have something to give back but don't go way over the top.

If someone gets abusive towards you, walk away. Do not lower yourself to their level. This can lead to no good and might even go against you if the issue goes legal.

Never, ever, ever get physical with another person! If they get physical with you report them to management or in some cases to the authorities. But do not respond with the same behavior. This can get you into trouble. Always take the high road and treat people with respect.

Always take names as you talk to people. Even if they have a name tag on I will ask them if I am pronouncing their names correctly. This will make them aware that I know their names. If you are in the escalation phase you might even write their name down on a piece of paper while still in front of them. This could be your way of telling them you know who they are and others will find out as well. Don't be obnoxious about it though. Just do it quietly.

Don't threaten people. This can get you into trouble if you are not careful. It might also get a company to hide behind their lawyers as well making any future resolution much more difficult. Try the nice approach at first and reserve threatening any other action for the latter stages of the process. Even then, never threaten anyone personally or you could wind up with much bigger problems.

Do not be afraid to escalate. If you are not getting anywhere with one person, try another. Your personalities might be a better fit than they were with the previous person.

Try to walk through the door calm and in control. It will help you communicate better and more effectively. If you are angry or upset, go for a walk and calm down. Then go to the store.

ALWAYS have alternatives in mind so when your demands are rejected you have a plan B and C ready. Don't rely on or expect others to come up with alternatives because they might not want to be bothered. But if you suggest them, they might agree.

Always come in with all your documentation. Don't expect others to look it up or find it for you. The easier you make it for people the more they will want to help you.

For more information on Customer Service please visit our website at:

http://www.allyouhavetoknow.com

(New website available in November of 2015)

Or visit the website of The Customer Service Training Institute at

http://www.infowhse.com

www.ingramcontent.com/pod-product-compliance
Lightning Source LLC
Chambersburg PA
CBHW051903170526
45168CB00001B/224